MACHIAVELLI
and the ART of
RENAISSANCE
HISTORY

Niccolò Machiavelli by Santi di Tito, *reprinted by permission of Vittorio Alinari, Florence.*

MACHIAVELLI
and the ART of
RENAISSANCE
HISTORY

Peter E. Bondanella

INDIANA UNIVERSITY

Wayne State University Press • Detroit • 1973

Published simultaneously in Canada
by the Copp Clark Publishing Company
517 Wellington Street, West
Toronto 2B, Canada.

Library of Congress Cataloging in Publication Data

Bondanella, Peter E   1943–
   Machiavelli and the art of Renaissance history.

   Includes bibliographical references.
   1. Machiavelli, Niccolò, 1469–1527.   I. Title.
DG738.14.M2B66 1973   914.5'03'60924 [B]   73–9729
ISBN 0–8143–1499–6

Publication of this book was assisted by the American Council of
Learned Societies under a grant from the Andrew W. Mellon Foundation.

For Julia

"La dompna es agradans e plazens,
per sa beutat la gardon mantas gens,
et a son cor en amar leyalmens."

Contents

Preface

One of the most striking characteristics of Machiavelli's works is his abiding interest in impressive figures of history, men whose exemplary actions or words aroused his quick imagination. The tendency to see historical events as the exclusive dominion of an active historical protagonist and to modify or reshape the description of such events in order better to portray the individual's distinctive traits is a basic element of Machiavelli's art. None of Machiavelli's writings are coldly abstract treatises on the nature of political power. All reflect the imagination with which their author was endowed. The important place Machiavelli gives in his works to the characterization of individuals who aroused his interest — actors on the stage of human history and examples, as he saw them, to be followed or avoided in one's political behavior — is one reason why his works attract contemporary readers. This interest first appears quite naturally with his writings ·from his first practical political experiences as an ambassador for the Florentine republic. His diplomatic correspondence shows in an embryonic form his descriptions of historical figures — Cesare Borgia, Pope Julius II, and Louis XII — who are later treated in his more famous works. It is there also that we can grasp several of the stylistic traits of Machiavelli's presentation of character.

Although concern with historical figures is always a dominant feature of his works from the early diplomatic letters to *The History of Florence,* the narrative techniques employed by Machiavelli to deal with his protagonists vary according to his purpose in each work. This study will analyze the way in which Machiavelli presents and examines his protagonists. The Florentine's contribution to the art of historical portraiture was more than simply a stylistic preoccupation, for in his works we see the rediscovery of the classical conception of the heroic character, best exemplified in analogous figures from classical epic or history. The continuity of Machiavelli's style in his many varied historical, political, and literary works has not often been noticed, and this work will analyze the purely fictional characters in Machiavelli's literary works to underline the stylistic similarities that exist between the protagonists of all of his writings. Machiavelli maintained a loose distinction between "historical" and "fictional" or "literary" characters. The portrait of the artist as he reveals himself in his personal letters will also be discussed. The inclusion of such a subject in a work on the art of Renaissance history is appropriate, for most writers of Machiavelli's day considered their personal letters both works of art and quasi-autobiographical documents intended to give posterity an insight into their personalities.

The purpose of this study is a literary one, and it is not intended to be an examination of Machiavelli's political thought except insofar as Machiavelli's theoretical ideas shape his portraits. Too many literary critics have allowed themselves to be carried from textual analyses of Machiavelli's prose into the realm of theoretical speculation upon a few "key" ideas which they believe inform all of his works. Since Machiavelli's prose is equal or superior to that of other Renaissance writers, it is only just that we examine his prose as we would that of Montaigne, Milton, Donne, or Bacon. Isolating this aspect of Machiavelli's works need not exclude questions of theoretical importance. On the contrary, an analysis of the importance of historical characters and Machiavelli's art of portraiture will add strength to the generaliza-

tions we can make about the conceptual universe of Machiavellian political thought.

Where possible, I have structured this study chronologically to give the reader some idea of the evolution of
Machiavelli's works and his style. Dates cited refer to ap-
proximate time of composition, not of publication, even
though some of these dates are impossible to determine ex-
actly and are still the subject of critical controversy. The
analysis of style in this work is based solely upon the Italian
texts. The English translations are provided to aid the non-
specialist who knows little or no Italian. My aim has been to
provide as literal a translation of the Italian texts as is possible.

My special thanks go to my wife Julia, to whom this
book is dedicated, and whose patience, advice, and skillful
corrections helped bring this study to fruition. I should also
like to express my appreciation to Professor Emmanel Hatz-
antonis, who first suggested this topic to me several years ago
and whose enthusiasm for Machiavelli was contagious; to
Professors Chandler B. Beall, Thomas R. Hart, Jr., and Andrea
di Tommaso, all of whom read parts of the manuscript at
various stages of its completion; and to my friends and former
colleagues in the Department of Romance and Germanic
Languages at Wayne State University, whose encouragement
and companionship made the completion of this study a pleas-
ant chore. A research grant-in-aid from Wayne State University enabled me to finish the manuscript in a proper Florentine setting, and for that I am deeply grateful. The editors of
Italica and *Forum Italicum* have generously permitted me to
reprint parts of previously published articles.

Abbreviations

ADG	Niccolò Machiavelli. *Arte della guerra e altri scritti politici.* Ed. Sergio Bertelli. Milan: Feltrinelli, 1961.
Approdo	*L'Approdo Letterario.*
BHR	*Bibliothèque d'Humanisme et Renaissance.*
FeL	*Filologia e Letteratura.*
FI	*Forum Italicum.*
GSLI	*Giornale Storico della Letteratura Italiana.*
IF	Niccolò Machiavelli. *Istorie fiorentine.* Ed. Franco Gaeta. Milan: Feltrinelli, 1962.
IQ	*Italian Quarterly.*
IS	*Italian Studies.*
JHI	*Journal of the History of Ideas.*
JWCI	*Journal of the Warburg and Courtauld Institute.*
KR	*Kenyon Review.*
KRQ	*Kentucky Romance Quarterly.*
L	Niccolò Machiavelli. *Lettere.* Ed. Franco Gaeta. Milan: Feltrinelli, 1961.
LC	Niccolò Machiavelli. *Legazioni e commissarie.* Ed. Sergio Bertelli. 3 vols. Milan: Feltrinelli, 1964.
LI	*Lettere Italiane.*
MLN	*Modern Language Notes.*
MP	*Modern Philology.*
NA	*Nuova Antologia.*
NRS	*Nuova Rivista Storica.*
PD	Niccolò Machiavelli. *Il Principe e Discorsi sopra la prima deca di Tito Livio.* Ed. Sergio Bertelli. Milan: Feltrinelli, 1968.
PMLA	*Publications of the Modern Language Association of America.*
RenQ	*Renaissance Quarterly.*
RNL	*Review of National Literatures.*
RR	*Romanic Review.*
TSL	Niccolò Machiavelli. *Il teatro e tutti gli scritti letterari.* Ed. Franco Gaeta. Milan: Feltrinelli, 1965.
UTQ	*University of Toronto Quarterly.*

I

The Literary Background of Machiavelli's Character Sketches

In a burst of enthusiasm, Francesco De Sanctis once claimed that Machiavelli's mind was so full of a new content that for him, content was everything and form was nothing: "not only does he do away with literary form, but he kills form in itself — and this in a century in which form was the only remaining God on the altars." [1] Although De Sanctis and successive generations of critics have emphasized Machiavelli's revolutionary political ideas, there is much of a traditional nature in the form of his works that they overlooked. Allan Gilbert has shown how *The Prince* stands in a long tradition of books written to instruct rulers on the proper functions of their offices.[2] The writing of commentaries on a classical text, the germinal idea of Machiavelli's *Discourses*, had been practiced throughout the classical and medieval periods. There exist, therefore, some obvious classical and medieval antecedents that could have guided Machiavelli in his preoccupation with historical figures and their mode of presentation in prose narrative. Given Machiavelli's classical bent, it was only natural that he looked to the writers of antiquity (mostly historians) for guidance.

Machiavelli could have read works of almost all the important Latin writers and many Greek authors accessible to him through Latin translations. These would include Livy, Cicero, Aristotle, Plutarch, Sallust, Tacitus, Thucydides, Xenophon, Diodorus Siculus, Juvenal, Polybius, Vegetius, Seneca.

Herodotus, and many lesser writers.[3] Critics who have examined the classical influence upon Machiavelli's works often
cannot identify specific sources, however, since Machiavelli
frequently cites stories and anecdotes which could have come
from a number of literary works, either classical originals or
medieval and Renaissance texts containing classical references.[4] Whatever his immediate source, Machiavelli's habit of
referring modern politics to his beloved Latin authors began
with his earliest works, long before his best known treatises,
The Prince and the *Discourses*, made the principle of imitation of the ancients a cardinal rule in his political philosophy.
In an early essay, *On the Method of Dealing with the Rebellious Peoples of the Valdichiana* (1503), Machiavelli opens
with a discussion of how the Roman senate reacted to an
uprising in one of its client states, a story he found in Livy's
From the Founding of the City (bk. 8). Only after presenting
this classical model does he turn to the question of a similar
revolt which Florence experienced. He recommends that
Florence follow the Roman example since "history is the
teacher of our actions, and especially of those of princes, and
the world has always been inhabited by men in the same
manner who have always possessed the same desires." [5] His
faith in the imitation of classical political practice is based
upon the assumption that man's nature is constant, and thus
men who study the past can learn from it, for the constancy
of human nature ensures that these ancient lessons can be
applied to modern politics.

   Machiavelli, without doubt a careful reader, must
have noticed how many classical writers concentrated upon
character sketches of important historical figures in their
works. H. D. Westlake makes a persuasive argument for the
importance of individuals in Thucydides' history of the Pelo-
ponnesian wars, examining the subtle manner in which Thucydides avoided explicit judgments upon his characters by
making his conclusions seem to arise naturally from the facts

he chose to report.[6] Thucydides' works were translated into Latin around 1485 so that Machiavelli had access to them. Though he refers to them several times in the *Discourses*,[7] Machiavelli was apparently not strongly influenced by Thucydides, and he seems to have treated his works as only a reservoir of stories from which he selected a few. The fact that the Greek historian characteristically avoided explicit judgments of his characters while Machiavelli usually became passionately involved with his own negates any important stylistic relationship between the two writers.

      Although Machiavelli's relationship to Thucydides is of little consequence in searching for antecedents to his interest in historical characters, his serious interest in and knowledge of both Livy and Plutarch are more significant. Livy was one of Machiavelli's favorite authors; his history of the city of Rome and of the exploits of "his" Romans, as Machiavelli affectionately called them, stressed historical individuals as the makers of history, for Livy regarded their particular personal traits (plus the added elements of chance and divine intervention) as the only elements necessary to explain the past. Livy's conception of history was dominated by idealized heroes and reprehensible villains, and his stress upon morally didactic history led him to falsify history by design, not by chance or error.[8] As we shall see later, Machiavelli also often distorts historical fact to create a good story or twists the truth to fit his own interpretation of events. Besides this general similarity in attitude toward historical "truth," many of Livy's stylistic characteristics can be found in Machiavelli's later historical works. These include fabricated literary speeches to give the reader an insight into the minds of the central characters, the *elogium* that summarizes a person's life and deeds after his death is described, or the use of anecdotes to epitomize a character's dominant traits.[9] Livy was, in the words of one scholar, the "didactic historian par excellence."[10] His own statement of purpose in the preface to the first book of his history of Rome is very close in spirit to Machiavelli's many exhortations to imitate classical antiquity in political practice:

What chiefly makes the study of history wholesome and profitable is this, that you behold the lessons of every kind of experience set forth as on a conspicuous monument; from these you may choose for yourself and for your own state what to imitate, from these mark for avoidance what is shameful in the conception and shameful in the result.[11]

As is evident from his declaration in *On the Method of Dealing with the Rebellious Peoples of the Valdichiana*, Machiavelli follows Livy in seeing history as a vast didactic process, but he differs from Livy in the kinds of lessons that can be learned from it. In an illuminating comparison of how both Livy (*From the Founding of the City*, bk. 8) and Machiavelli (*Discourses*, bk. 3, ch. 22) describe the execution of the Consul Titus Manlius's son on the father's own orders because of his son's disobedience, William S. Anderson concludes:

Machiavelli removes all moral qualities from this situation and every situation, and where Livy's history constitutes a moral interpretation of Roman greatness, the Florentine searches for a nonmoral, realistic explanation of success. Machiavelli's insight makes of history an objective concantenation of facts, capable of teaching the *practical* statesman how to create a powerful state regardless of ethical criteria.[12]

While Anderson tends to repeat the shopworn idea that Machiavelli completely ignores moral considerations in his political universe, his distinction between moral and practical exempla is a useful one. Machiavelli may have learned from Livy how to use history as an educational tool, but he had his own specifically "Machiavellian" rules of conduct for which he sought to provide historical evidence, and thus, he approaches his characters from an essentially different point of view.

Of all the classical authors that Machiavelli had read, the one whose passion for the study of historical figures best matches Machiavelli's was Plutarch. Although Plutarch became the vogue of the educated European reader after Machiavelli's day, there was nevertheless ample opportunity for Machiavelli to read his *Parallel Lives* (otherwise known as *The Lives of the Noble Grecians and Romans*). Latin editions of his collections of biographical sketches appeared as early as 1470 in Italy;[13] an Italian translation was made by Jaconello in 1488, long before North or Amyot published their more famous versions.[14] Many of the historical events reported in the *Discourses*, in fact, come from Plutarch rather than Livy.[15] A letter from Biagio Buonaccorsi to Machiavelli dated 21 October 1502 testifies to Machiavelli's enthusiasm for Plutarch's works: "We have searched everywhere for Plutarch's *Lives*, and we cannot find a copy in Florence. Have patience, since it is necessary to write to Venice; and to tell you the truth, you are a bother to request so many things." [16] It is interesting that Machiavelli makes this request for a copy of Plutarch's works during the time he is in Imola on a diplomatic mission to Cesare Borgia. At the very moment when the prototype of the modern military hero is before him "in flesh and bone," as Federico Chabod puts it,[17] Machiavelli seeks to examine the heroes of classical antiquity through the medium of Plutarch's works. Perhaps Borgia reminded Machiavelli of one of Plutarch's characters, and he wanted to refresh his memory by a rereading of the work. Perhaps Machiavelli already envisioned writing a work on Borgia's life and wanted to follow the manner of Plutarch's famous biographies. No answer to such speculation is possible, since none of Machiavelli's many character sketches of Borgia reflect the direct influence of Plutarch. The fact that Machiavelli had both Borgia and Plutarch on his mind at a crucial point in his intellectual development suggests at least the general influence of Plutarch upon Machiavelli's art of portraiture, since among classical writers, Plutarch most successfully used biographical sketches as models for imitation.

Both Plutarch and Machiavelli embodied in historical characters abstract conceptions which represented standards of conduct that they were to promote as exemplary to all of modern Europe. However, Plutarch's interest in individuals was closer to that of Livy. Like Livy, he stressed the moral qualities of his exempla:

It was for the sake of others that I first commenced writing biographies; but I find myself proceeding and attaching myself to it for my own; the virtues of these great men serving me as a sort of looking-glass, in which I may see how to adjust and adorn my own life. . . . what more effective means to one's moral improvement? [18]

Machiavelli was more interested in the practical or political lessons to be gained from the imitation of the men Plutarch or Livy had presented for very different reasons, but in his greatest works he often used similar stylistic techniques — especially that of using anecdotes or small details of a man's life to portray his innermost character. In Plutarch's life of Alexander the Great, this practice is explained clearly:

And the most glorious exploits do not always furnish us with the clearest discoveries of virtue and vice in men; sometimes a matter of less moment, an expression or a jest, informs us better of their characters and inclinations, than the most famous sieges, the greatest armaments, or the bloodiest battles whatsoever. Therefore as portrait-painters are more exact in the lines and features of the face, in which the character is seen, than in the other parts of the body, so I must be allowed to give my more particular attention to the marks and inclinations of the souls of men.[19]

The avowed purpose of narrative prose for most ancient historians or biographers was a rhetorical one, that of persuasion. As Cicero put it, "history is a branch of study which is predominantly the concern of the orator." [20] Since the aim of the moralist was to teach, persuade, and guide, it was "inevitable that ancient historians, who wanted to exercise the moralist's persuasion, were powerfully affected by rhetoric." [21] One of the most effective persuasive devices or techniques that either the orator or the historian had at his disposal was the figure of the exemplum. If persuasion was their goal, exempla, or illustrative examples of points under discussion, were a good means of proving a point. A whole tradition stressing this simple device grew up in the ancient schools of rhetoric; the device was applied to prose narrative (especially history), and it later influenced both Christian pulpit oratory and prose fiction for many years. Collections of stories like Boccaccio's *Decameron,* which Machiavelli surely knew, were distant cousins of the exemplum, because each story and character sketch could be read as an illustration of a type of character.[22] Even more obviously connected with this rhetorical tradition were the various early Latin works by Italians which treated historical or legendary characters in a biographical manner, presenting them as exempla to imitate or to avoid. The best known of such books are Petrarch's *Concerning Famous Men (De viris illustribus)* and Boccaccio's *Concerning Famous Women (De claris mulieribus)* and *The Fates of Illustrious Men (De casibus virorum illustrium).* In each of these works, biographical sketches of famous men or women from history and legend (many of them the same people who fascinated Machiavelli) were held up for examination by the reader. These Latin works had an early and profound influence upon Renaissance Europe, and Machiavelli could not have failed to have some knowledge of them.[23] Livy was a major source for both Boccaccio and Petrarch, however, and Machiavelli could have read many of the stories from these Latin works in the original source. Such works presented exempla in the service of the traditional Christian morality and normally presented historical or legendary characters solely for moral instruction. A good example of the distance that separates the political, practical illustrations of Machiavelli and those of Petrarch or Boccaccio is Boccaccio's treatment of Walter, the Duke of Athens, in *The Fates of Illustrious Men*. This petty tyrant serves Machiavelli as the model of the overweening ruler and inspires the most memorable and dramatic passage in *The History of Florence*. This passage will be examined in greater detail in the chapter devoted to that work. Boccaccio removes all of the drama and the political implications from his account which he, like Machiavelli, probably found in Villani's chronicle of Florentine history. For him, Walter serves as an exemplum of divine justice and providence inherent in human history, and the Florentine revolt against Walter is essentially founded upon heavenly intervention rather than upon political motives: "Finally God had compassion on their undeserved plight and permitted their eyes to be opened, so they could see the unhappiness of their base servitude. With His strength He made their flickering hearts firm. . . . Oh, Heavenly Father, how marvelous are thy judgments!" [24] Machiavelli's best character sketches always avoid the strict moral exemplarism of these Latin works. They are portraits of concrete historical individuals who assume symbolic roles in Machiavelli's literary universe without losing their historical identity, in much the same way that Dante's *Comedy* presents historical individuals who also function as symbols of sin or virtue.

Another important tradition influential in shaping Machiavelli's attitudes toward history and its protagonists was the humanist historiography that had long been associated with the Florentine Chancellery when Machiavelli entered it in 1498. The humanists of the early Renaissance had attempted to revive the ancient art of history, taking Livy as their principal model for their favorite project — the history of their own city-state. Both Leonardo Bruni (1374–1444) and Poggio Bracciolini (1380–1459), for instance, served as head of the Florentine Chancellery, and both wrote Latin histories of their native city. Genoa, Milan, Bologna, and Verona all had humanists of lesser importance who attempted to rival Livy in chronicling the story of their respective towns. The Florentine humanists often found their historical information in medieval chronicles such as those written by Villani or Compagni, but they closely followed the general principles of organization and style learned from their classical masters.[25] Machiavelli's last major work, *The History of Florence,* was written in this humanist tradition. As Felix Gilbert has noted, Machiavelli used the humanist pattern of writing history as a framework onto which he hung his political message: "Machiavelli adhered to the humanist principle that 'history teaches by example,' only the 'examples' which Machiavelli adduced were intended to demonstrate the existence and the functioning of political laws." [26]

In the preamble to *The History of Florence,* Machiavelli discusses the humanist tradition and characterizes the works of his predecessors. He admits that both Bruni and Bracciolini are "two excellent historians," but he feels that their narration of Florentine external affairs is far superior to their discussion of the internal political conflicts that had always been at the center of the city's history:

I found that in describing the wars carried on by the Florentines with foreign princes and peoples they were very diligent historians, but concerning civil discord and internal conflicts, and the effects these have caused, they are totally silent about one part of them, and the other they describe so briefly that their readers can derive no profit or pleasure.[27]

This last phrase, "profit or·pleasure" ("utile o piacere alcuno"), emphasizes the twin aspects that history always had for classical and humanist historians. History was first of all a didactic means of communication (*utile*). Its purpose was to teach men how to conduct their affairs properly by providing models to imitate or to avoid. But it was also a literary genre (*piacere*) in which a pleasing style was just as important as the search for strict historical "truth." The fact that Machiavelli underlines these two characteristics of history may strike the modern reader as a betrayal of the basic goal of the historian, but the modern emphasis upon research guided by a desire to uncover factual truth is a relatively new concept in historiography.[28] For Machiavelli, history is essentially an educational tool that is also a pleasurable, literary genre with its own proper style and principles of organization. Indeed, it is the pleasing form of presentation that alone guarantees the impact of the moral lesson. This combination of the useful and the pleasurable is only another version of the great commonplace definition of the end of literature itself, best expressed in and often quoted from the works of Horace. Machiavelli took the definition seriously, however, and the fact that he considered history to be a literary pursuit explains in part his great attention to the art of portraiture.

Besides these various strains of classical and humanist historiography, more specifically fictional works may also have influenced Machiavelli's interest in great men. The depiction of the hero was an established literary *topos* in classical, medieval, and Renaissance epic literature.[29] Such epic figures as Aeneas, Achilles, and Odysseus were seen as more than military leaders. They were viewed as ideal figures, embodiments of nobility whose characters and deeds made them models for educating and inspiring men of other ages.[30] Machiavelli most certainly knew Virgil's *Aeneid,* and his close association with Marcello Virgilio Adriani (his teacher, superior in the Chancellery, and one of the first Italian commentators on the *Iliad*), possibly gave him access to Homer's works.[31] Besides these ancient literary heroes, Machiavelli had medieval precedents for the study of the deeds of great men. The adulation of the warrior or prince was not unknown in the Middle Ages, in spite of Burckhardt's often quoted assertion that hero worship is a typically Renaissance phenomenon, and such an attitude found its medieval expression in many literary biographies of the perfect knight.[32]

Thus, Machiavelli had at least three different but related historical traditions at his disposal. He may also have been influenced by classical and medieval literary presentations of heroic protagonists. He knew the major classical historians, and their didactic brand of history with its emphasis upon exemplary characters had a strong impact upon his works. The tradition of historiography which flourished in the Florentine Chancellery and which was an outgrowth of the classical tradition provided Machiavelli with much of the framework for *The History of Florence*. The tradition represented by the Latin works of Petrarch and Boccaccio was the least congenial to his own sensibility. Machiavelli's historical exempla are usually placed in a dynamic environment of political activity surrounded by a theoretical framework of his own political ideas; they are rarely presented as historical personifications of simple vice or virtue.

Though Machiavelli had a rich literary background upon which to draw for character portraiture, we must look to his own observation, his own political experience, and his lively creative imagination for the genesis of his character sketches. In his earliest works (the letters he composed as a young emissary of the Florentine republic between 1498 and 1512), we can detect an unusual attitude which we can only define as a literary approach to historical figures of his own day. An examination of the diplomatic correspondence will show how his early political experiences led to his first literary character sketches, even if those sketches lack the comprehensive theoretical framework that guided his purpose in his more mature works. The characters he describes in these letters — Cesare Borgia, Pope Julius II, King Louis XII, and many others — become key figures in his later, more famous works.

II *The Diplomatic Correspondence: Embryonic Sketches and Impetuous Judgments*

In a recent study of Machiavelli's diplomatic correspondence during his first three years in the Florentine Chancellery (July 1498 until July 1501), Fredi Chiappelli has shown how many of the characteristics of Machiavelli's mature style — his habit of stating propositions in their polar extremes, the frequent use of Latinisms, the constant tendency to seek general rules of human conduct, even the vivid imagery — can be found *in nuce* in these early documents.[1] The popular view that Machiavelli was primarily a practical politician who only developed an interest in writing to pass the time after his abrupt exile from the Chancellery in 1512 is therefore false, but it is an opinion so widespread that it is partially responsible for the fact that many of Machiavelli's writings in the Chancellery remain unpublished.[2] There is a unity in Machiavelli's thought and style that spans the date of his exile from politics, a continuity which no longer permits scholars to speak of Machiavelli the secretary and Machiavelli the political theorist as if they were two separate personalities. Scholars have only begun to examine the relationships between these early diplomatic papers and the later works which form Machiavelli's reputation, but students of diplomatic history have long esteemed Machiavelli's concise, informative correspondence as masterpieces. Although most diplomats of the period in the Florentine government viewed the avoidance of personal opinion in their dispatches as a fixed rule based upon classical precedent,[3] Machiavelli was often unable to constrain himself. His impatience with the Florentine policy of temporizing often appears in his dispatches, even though he sometimes ends his impetuous personal judgments with phrases like "only time, the father of truth, will tell." [4] Machiavelli often gave unsolicited advice to his superiors. For instance, in a letter written while he was at Cesare Borgia's court in Imola, he says: "I have nothing more to write to your Lordships, unless it be that if I were asked for my opinion of all these movements [i.e., giving aid to Borgia], I would reply *praestita venia.*" [5] In this case, the Latin phrase (meaning "show favor" or "support") even draws attention to Machiavelli's unorthodox advice. After reading this report on Borgia from Imola, his good friend Biagio Buonaccorsi told Machiavelli that "sometimes you are too hasty in your conclusions when you write." [6] But, as Machiavelli saw it, diplomats had a patriotic duty to report the truth and to offer advice even if it was unwanted: "And if we have expressed ourselves too boldly, it is because we preferred to write and to be in error rather than to fail to write, thus harming ourselves instead of failing in our duty to the republic." [7]

Machiavelli's attempts to express his personal opinion about each historical figure he encounters on his missions are important, for the nature of diplomatic correspondence left him little room to practice portraiture for the sake of portraiture. In fact, in all of his dispatches, there are no character sketches that match in artistic sophistication those of his later works. However, he does present what we might call preliminary drafts or notes for sketches, observations which may be later expanded into more highly wrought literary portraits. Such remarks reveal Machiavelli's interest in the basic qualities of these men, attributes of their characters which make them act as they do and thus make their behavior predictable. Years later Machiavelli advised a friend who was about to embark upon a mission to Spain, Raffaello Girolami, that such observations were a diplomat's business: "And to come to particulars, I say that you have to observe the nature of the man; whether he governs himself or allows himself to be ruled, whether he is avaricious or generous, whether he loves war or peace, whether he has a passion for glory or anything else." [8] This attempt to explore the character of his subjects is a major preoccupation of his diplomatic writings and is continued in all his later works. Such observations do not result in highly artistic literary portraits in the dispatches, but they do show Machiavelli's tendency to seek out a man's inner qualities that will characterize all of his greatest character sketches. Since many of the same figures are presented in other works, an examination of Machiavelli's "light-handed" drafts and his often impetuous personal judgments in the dispatches is important in studying his art of portraiture.

Machiavelli completed four missions to the court of Louis XII (1500, 1503, 1510, and 1511). The major trait of this monarch's personality, reported in all of Machiavelli's dispatches from these missions, is his miserly nature, a characteristic Machiavelli then believed was totally unbecoming to a great leader.[9] Machiavelli always connects this trait with an astute political observation; he does not comment on the king's personality simply to fill up space but constantly looks for those qualities that could explain the king's political actions. His first remark on Louis shows how this miserly nature blinds the king to the undertaking of great deeds — "the king's nature concerning the spending of funds," Machiavelli notes, makes him ever anxious "to draw all he can from this country but never willing to spend anything there, seeming to think more about present convenience than that which might result of it later." [10] This avariciousness is not just a minor quirk, but it is a clue to the central fact about him that an ally or an adversary should know — his obsession with immediate, short-range advantages blinds him to the potentialities of ambitious, long-range goals. To strengthen his own evaluation, Machiavelli reports what appears to be a conversation with one of the king's courtiers who said that Louis was "very, very prudent; that his ears were long, but his belief short; that he listened to everything but put faith only in what he could touch with his hands and prove true." [11] Whether or not such a conversation actually took place is impossible to determine, but the conversations or speeches in Machiavelli's dispatches too often agree with his own opinions to be considered verbatim reports. It is hard not to see Machiavelli's own bias as the motivation for the sarcastic use of the word "prudentissima" or for the biting remark that the king fails to understand anything but what he can touch. A more unflattering description of a monarch's capacity for political imagination could not be reported in so few words.

Louis's political vision is so shortsighted that he insists upon the defense of his own personal honor even at the expense of his Florentine allies. Machiavelli's passion is clearly aroused by Louis's failure to see that forcing Florence against the pope could mean only disaster for the city, even though it might satisfy the king's overdeveloped sense of honor. Commenting on this, Machiavelli uses his classic "dilemma-like" technique of emphasizing the extremes when he says: "Whether waking or sleeping, the king neither thinks nor dreams of anything but the wrong which he imagines he has received at the hands of the pope, and his mind is filled with nothing but thoughts of vendetta." [12] Such an alliance, as Machiavelli indignantly describes it, would render the Florentines "unarmed in the midst of their enemies." [13] It is not a coincidence that Machiavelli later uses the same word with the same passionate tone in discussing Savonarola in *The Prince*: "From this comes the fact that armed prophets conquered and unarmed prophets came to ruin." [14] In reporting the death of Cardinal Georges d'Amboise, Louis's expert diplomat, Machiavelli makes a lucid comparison of his political skill and that of the king:

For the king is not accustomed to attend to the details of all these things and neglects them, while those whose duty it is to attend to them take no authority upon themselves either to act or to remind the king what he ought to do; and so, while the physician gives no thought to the sick patient, and the assistant forgets him, the patient dies. During the time while I was talking with Robertet today, a painter who carried a portrait of the late Cardinal d'Amboise came in, which caused Robertet to exclaim with a sigh: "O, my master, if you were still living, we should now be with our army in Rome!" These words confirmed me more fully in all that I write to you above.[15]

This extended metaphor depicting the cardinal as a skillful surgeon, the king as a careless, amateur hospital attendant, and the delicate Italian situation as a dying patient is one of Machiavelli's earliest uses of medical imagery to refer to politics, imagery better known from *The Prince*.[16] In only a few sentences, Machiavelli has captured the king's nature. It is the nucleus of a portrait, a description with a literary flourish, a compelling metaphor that has more force than a simple declaration of the king's incompetence. It is proof that Machiavelli viewed even his diplomatic dispatches as a quasi-literary medium and consciously used his artistic skill to present his opinions in as pleasing a form as possible. In four separate missions to France, Machiavelli's dispatches display a consistently negative evaluation of the French monarch. The king's miserly nature serves Machiavelli as a clue to his general blindness, his incapacity to come to grips with great political questions because of his concentration upon the "present convenience."

An interesting parallel to the picture of King Louis XII is Machiavelli's brief treatment of Emperor Maximilian in dispatches from a mission to Germany in 1507. Maximilian seemed to Machiavelli the polar opposite of the French king; instead of being miserly, he was overgenerous and credulous. Again, the observation of this trait is connected with a political observation — his extravagant ways always leave the emperor devoid of resources to carry out his ambitious plans:

No one doubts that the Emperor has plenty of soldiers which are of good quality; but of how he will keep them together, there is the doubt. For he can only hold them by means of money; and being, on the one hand, short of cash himself, he can never be sure that it will be supplied by others; and, on the other hand, being extremely liberal, he adds difficulty to difficulty; and although generosity is a virtue in princes, yet it is not enough to satisfy one thousand when there are twenty thousand more who are in need.[17]

Machiavelli concludes that the emperor's plans in Italy will come to no avail: "But he is so good and humane a lord that he has become too easy and too credulous, whence it comes that some people have grave doubts as to the success of his enterprise, as I have stated above." [18] Here, as in the description of Louis XII as a "prudent" man, Machiavelli uses two ordinarily complimentary words ("good" and "humane") in such a way as to indicate that these qualities are not virtues within his own system of political morality but are almost synonyms for the derogatory words "easy" and "credulous." The majority of the dispatches from this German mission were signed by Francesco Vettori (the ranking diplomat on the mission), even though most were written either partially or completely by Machiavelli, a situation similar to that of the mission to France of Della Casa and Machiavelli in 1500.[19] Some scholars refuse to see any difference between the ideas or style of Vettori and Machiavelli. J. R. Hale, for example, says that it is "seldom profitable to distinguish between the opinions of the two men," and that the style of one is not easily separate from the other.[20] In the dispatch quoted above containing the brief reference to the emperor's "nature," it is significant, in the light of Hale's refusal to distinguish between Machiavelli and Vettori (an opinion not shared by Bertelli, the editor of the dispatches) that the letter is actually composed by both men. The part of the letter describing the emperor's nature is entirely in Machiavelli's hand, while the section in Vettori's hand is singularly without literary interest.[21] When Machiavelli's imprint is visible in a dispatch, he follows the precept he gave to Raffaello Girolami: his characteristic interest in defining the "nature" of his historical protagonists is usually evident.

Other important dispatches refer to Cesare Borgia and Pope Julius II. The actions of both men left an indelible impression on Machiavelli's imagination, and it was no wonder that these striking figures were later used in key passages of both *The Prince* and the *Discourses*. Machiavelli's treatment of Borgia in the diplomatic correspondence often prefigures the famous chapter seven of *The Prince*, but his style of presentation in the letters differs significantly from that chapter and from several other minor essays. Machiavelli observed Borgia during three missions — at Urbino (1502), at Imola (1502–1503), and at Rome (1503). The Urbino letters bear only the signature of Francesco Soderini, even though both Machiavelli and Soderini composed them.[22] All of the letters from the other two missions bear Machiavelli's signature, and his constant attempt to capture the Duke's "nature" and to explain his actions in terms of it in these two series of dispatches is further evidence of his authorship.

The awesome impression Borgia made upon Machiavelli and Soderini at Urbino after having captured the city without a struggle is evident from the report of their first encounter with the Duke. The setting is described with a high sense of drama. The two men are summoned into a heavily guarded palace at two o'clock in the morning, the time and place being intended to intimidate them. This is how Borgia's first speech is reported:

His Lordship, without circumlocutions, said: ". . . I know too well that your city is not well disposed towards me; on the contrary, Florence would drop me like an assassin if she could, and she has tried to create large problems for me both with the Pope and with the king of France." The last part of his words we denied, and we disproved the other with our explanations. He said: "I know very well that you are prudent and that you understand me; therefore, I shall repeat myself to you in a few words. This government in Florence does not please me, and you must guarantee the observance of what you have promised me: otherwise you will understand in a very short time that I do not wish to live in this manner; and if you do not wish me as a friend, you will find me an enemy." [23]

It is not likely that Machiavelli and Soderini had pen and paper at hand during this tense moment to take down Borgia's exact words. The dramatic setting and the style of Borgia's "few words" themselves — very close to Machiavelli's own tendency to emphasize the extremes of a situation ("and if you do not wish me as a friend, you will find me an enemy") — indicate that the Florentine may have added his own touch to the speech as he was later to do in many imaginary speeches in his historical works to strengthen the impression that Borgia would make on his readers in the Chancellery. In another passage, Machiavelli describes Borgia's nature as revealed by his feats:

This lord is very splendid and magnificent, and is so courageous in arms that even the greatest undertaking appears small to him, and both for the acquisition of glory and for more territory he never rests nor recognizes weariness nor danger. In battle he arrives at a place before one can even realize that his men have been moved; he has hired the best soldiers in Italy. All of which make him victorious and formidable together with his perpetual good fortune.[24]

In this passage, we have a germinal definition of the term *virtù* and its connection to *fortuna*, a key element in Machiavelli's great political works. Mark Musa notes that *virtù* is coupled with *fortuna* seventeen times in *The Prince* and "in every such coupling it can be translated in its broader meaning of 'ingenuity.'" [25] Here, the major portion of the description of Borgia's nature underlines his ingenuity — as Musa defines it, a Machiavellian quality which "combines aptness and skill with inventive power and cleverness in originating and contriving." [26] The conjunction of these two qualities in the person of Cesare Borgia (*fortuna* mentioned explicitly, *virtù* implicitly) presents one of the main tenets of Machiavellian thought, that a successful prince must know how to act immediately and decisively and must furthermore have the favor of fortune to mold political events to his purposes.

The picture of Borgia at Imola anticipates the tone of Machiavelli's later remarks about him in *The Prince*. The rhetoric of presentation comes very close to Machiavelli's later usage of Borgia in that work as an exemplum, for he is introduced in that particular style which Charles Singleton sees as the key to Machiavelli's dialectics in his greatest works.[27] The indefinite pronoun *chi* ("whoever") introduces a statement in such a way that the reader is invited to accept the statement as a general truth without questioning its premises:

And whoever examines the characters of both the one and the other party will find in the Duke a daring and fortunate man, full of hope, and favored by a pope and a king; a man who finds himself assailed by others, not only in a state that he wishes to acquire but also in the one he has already acquired.[28]

Particular events are reported, not because of Machiavelli's desire to communicate faithfully each detail of the action to the Chancellery, but because of their usefulness in symbolizing the powerful personality of the man who initiated them. For example, Machiavelli uses the sudden discovery of Borgia's execution of his trusted lieutenant Remirro de Orco to show the arbitrary nature of Borgia's personal power.[29] This terrible aspect of the Duke's nature is even clearer in Machiavelli's account of Borgia's treachery at Sinigaglia. The most dramatic part of the story is the portrait of Vitellozzo's arrival into Borgia's trap:

Vitellozzo came mounted on a little mule, unarmed, with a patched coat, black and worn, and on top of it another black coat lined with green, and whoever saw him would never have judged him to be the man who twice that year tried to drive the King of France from Italy. His look was pale and dumbfounded, a trait which denoted easily to everyone watching his future death.[30]

With his emphasis upon Vitellozzo's faded black garments and pale face, Machiavelli fashions the man's physical appearance so that it underlines his fate as a kind of sacrificial lamb being led to slaughter. The motivation of the physical details is purely symbolic; these are cleverly used by Machiavelli to portray the state of mind of the captured man and to foreshadow his execution. One critic has called this passage a small masterpiece of psychological insight, one of the few times that Machiavelli uses visible details to portray psychological states.[31] While I agree with the first part of his description, I find that this type of symbolic assessment of physical details occurs in such works as *The History of Florence* and *The Life of Castruccio Castracani of Lucca*. In both of these major works, striking examples of such a technique are to be found and will be examined later.

In the dispatches from Rome, Machiavelli's presentation and appraisal of Borgia change abruptly; the superhuman figure he had presented at Urbino and Imola, the man endowed with *virtù* and the favor of *fortuna*, now becomes almost an object of scorn. What was once Borgia's greatest quality, his resoluteness, is precisely the quality that is now undermined by his change of fortune with the death of his father, Pope Alexander VI. Machiavelli again uses the conversations of others to report his own opinions. The prelate of Volterra finds Borgia "changed, irresolute, suspicious, and unstable in all his conclusions." [32] The Bishop of Elna is even more graphic in describing the change in Borgia's nature: "the duke seemed to him to have lost his wits, for he appeared not to know himself or what he wanted, so confused and irresolute was he." [33] Such a change in Borgia's bearing must have astonished Machiavelli after he had previously seen so many praiseworthy qualities in him. Although his future evaluation of Borgia in *The Prince* remains a favorable one, in this dispatch Machiavelli was too close to his subject for even a partially objective judgment. He has seen that his idol has feet of clay, and his observations take on a bitter, sarcastic tone. Whereas he once marveled at Borgia's cleverness at Sinigaglia, he now gloats over Borgia's stupidity in allowing a Rovere to be elected pope:

For the pope's innate hatred of him is notorious. And it is not to be supposed that Julius II will so quickly have forgotten the ten years of exile which he had to endure under Pope Alexander VI. The duke meanwhile allows himself to be carried away by his self-confidence, believing that the word of others is more to be relied upon than his own.[34]

Borgia has committed the cardinal "sin" in Machiavelli's new system of political morality; he has put more trust in a man's word than he ought to have done, more, certainly, than his knowledge of Renaissance politics should have allowed him to do. As Machiavelli lowers Borgia in his estimation, he raises his adversary, Pope Julius II, to take the duke's former place in his esteem. The pope's impetuous nature struck the same responsive chord that had originally drawn Machiavelli to Borgia. When Machiavelli learns of a rumor that Pope Julius has had Borgia thrown into the Tiber River, his remarks reveal his sarcastic disdain for a loser: "and now we see how honorably this pope begins to pay his debts, and how he wipes them out as with a blotter. Nevertheless, everyone blesses his hands and will do so still more, the more decidedly he goes ahead." [35] Washing his hands of a failure, Machiavelli declares that Borgia is no longer worthy of consideration: "and since the duke is taken, whether dead or alive, we can now act without thinking anymore about him." [36] In a final remark, he says that "we see now that the duke's sins have little by little brought him to penitence." [37] It is not in jest that Machiavelli uses religious terms to refer to Borgia's fall. Since his hero has broken the unwritten but immutable rules of politics by putting more trust in the words of others than in his own strength, he has to pay for his "sin" by the "penitence" of political defeat.

One critic, Gennaro Sasso, has criticized the image of Borgia in the Urbino dispatches, calling it marred by a static quality because of Machiavelli's desire to sketch a hero modeled upon classical analogs; in contrast, he finds that the image of Borgia in the other two collections of dispatches from Imola and Rome shows him to be a political model or symbol rather than a literary or rhetorical creation.[38] Sasso is more interested in arriving at Machiavelli's judgment of Borgia in *The Prince* than he is in carrying out a textual or stylistic analysis of the diplomatic dispatches. Consequently, he uses the term "literary" or "rhetorical" in a derogatory manner. Sasso is, moreover, incorrect in assuming that the so-called "static" quality he observes in the Urbino letters is caused by the artistic impulse to sketch a literary, rhetorical portrait of Borgia, an impulse that he feels is replaced by a presumably nonliterary (and political) purpose in the other dispatches from Imola and Rome. The simplest explanation for the difference between the Urbino dispatches and those of Imola and Rome is that Machiavelli alone composed these later dispatches. He had no superior's opinions to hamper his own expression of opinion and his own style.[39] It is not a changing purpose Sasso detects but a change in authorship; Borgia becomes a more interesting character in the last two dispatches because Machiavelli, true to his own precepts, has concentrated upon the innermost qualities of the duke's nature or character.

Machiavelli's art of portraiture in his diplomatic correspondence is in an embryonic state. Such a medium as a diplomatic letter did not allow him the fullest possible expression of his literary talents, although what we might term "rough drafts" of character sketches are certainly evident in his treatment of Louis XII and Cesare Borgia. Furthermore, he was in the process of developing his political ideas during this early period, ideas which would later be used to give a theoretical framework to many of the same characters and situations in more mature works which would be written without the constricting form of what was essentially a business letter. It is evident, however, that Machiavelli did not simply report events as they happened. Even in such a nonliterary medium as a diplomatic letter, he often includes a vivid metaphor or a stylized speech which is designed to illuminate the innermost qualities of the historical figure under examination. These early letters are important, for they reveal tendencies in his style and thought that were more fully developed in his mature art of portraiture. He remains fascinated with many of the same figures throughout his life. They reappear many times in his other works, often with greater emphasis upon style and less upon simple definition of their "nature." The moral or intellectual qualities of a man that interest Machiavelli are those which determine practical political success, not those which lead to a virtuous life. His tendency to judge characters on the basis of his own political morality rather than on the basis of traditional ethics is already evident in these letters. Men like Borgia who fail have "sinned" and must undergo punishment. The only real sin in Machiavelli's opinion, at this time as well as in his later works, is failure. Although symbolic physical details are rare in his dispatches, the way he uses them in the picture of Vitellozzo at Sinigaglia shows that Machiavelli has already mastered this technique. Only when Machiavelli combined his efforts to examine the innermost nature of an historical figure (already observable in the dispatches) with greater attention to the literary presentation of such characters within a broader theoretical framework than was possible in diplomatic correspondence would his art of portraiture emerge as a major aspect of his prose style. In the dispatches, although his observations and judgments are often important, they represent only embryonic portraits, the product of a young writer whose impetuous judgments were not matched by an equal attention to the style of their presentation.

III The Minor Writings: Transitional Bridges to the Great Political Works

Machiavelli wrote many minor works during his tenure in the Florentine Chancellery, short essays which grew out of these diplomatic experiences. The preceding chapter discussed Machiavelli's attempts to examine the personalities of several key historical figures, to fathom, as he put it in his letter to Raffaello Girolami, "the nature of the man." In his minor works, Machiavelli continues this preoccupation but mixes it with other considerations. In some of these short essays, he extends the focus of the dispatches, sketching the "nature" of his characters and even expanding his analysis to include the characteristics of an entire nation. Such a focus did not favor a highly developed art of portraiture, since any such art of necessity would, in literature as in the plastic arts, concentrate upon individuals rather than abstract groups.

In the dispatches, Machiavelli had given much attention to the French king and little to the German emperor. In these essays, he reverses the process, treating the emperor at length and studying the French national traits in more depth. The picture of Maximilian here agrees with that in the dispatches. In *Report on Germany* (1508), Machiavelli echoes his general assessment of the emperor in his letters: "these two qualities, liberality and the facility of his character, which others praise in him are the very traits that ruin him." [1] In the dispatches, Machiavelli had called the emperor "good" and "humane," ironically using these terms to connote derogatory judgments. In his *Report on Germany*, he makes explicit this negative evaluation. Machiavelli still admits that the man has admirable qualities, since he is a perfect soldier, he governs with great justice, and he has many of the required attributes of the perfect ruler. It is clear, however, that Machiavelli doubts that the emperor can ever rise above his gullible nature. In a comment on a remark made by one of the emperor's courtiers to the effect that any man or anything could fool him at least once, Machiavelli sarcastically notes: "but there are so many men and so many things, that he is exposed every day to being deceived, even if he were constantly on his guard." [2] In the *Discourse on Germany and the Emperor* (1509), he repeats this judgment in a paragraph beautifully constructed on antitheses to capture perfectly the emperor's contradictory nature:

I shall limit myself only to remarks about the emperor's nature: there is not, and perhaps never has been, a prince more wasteful of his resources than he. This explains why he is always in want, and why he never has money enough, no matter in what situation he may find himself. He is capricious, since he wants one thing today and forgets it tomorrow; he takes advice from no one, and yet believes everyone; he desires what he cannot have, and rejects that which he could obtain, and therefore he always makes contradictory resolutions. . . . He is humane in his audiences, but will grant them only at his leisure; he does not like ambassadors to pay him court unless he sends for them; he is extremely secretive; he lives in a constant state of agitation of mind and body, but he often undoes in the evening what he has concluded in the morning.[3]

In the *Description of German Affairs* (1512–1513), Machiavelli also judges the nature of the entire German people, and his opinion — repeated almost verbatim from the earlier *Report on Germany* — is not far removed from the modern stereotype of the industrious, frugal German worker. The national traits contrast with the profligacy of the German ruler:

The reason why the German citizens are rich is that they live as if they were poor; they do not build, and spend nothing on clothing or costly furniture in their houses. They are satisfied with having plenty of bread and meat, and a stove where they can take refuge from the cold. . . . And thus they enjoy their rough life and liberty.[4]

Rather than reflecting an accurate portrait of the German people here, Machiavelli seems instead to be borrowing from the famous description of the German people by Tacitus in his older history of the German tribes.[5] Like Tacitus, who contrasted the vigorous simplicity of those tribes to the corruption of Rome, Machiavelli associates the rough and essentially unpolished nature of their culture with their freedom and contrasts it to the civilized city-states of Italy, each dominated by petty tyrants.

Machiavelli's attempts to formulate outlines of national characteristics are most evident in works referring to his experiences in France. In the *Description of French Affairs* (1512–1513), he says that the French are "by nature more ferocious than vigorous and skillful," or that "the Frenchman is naturally covetous of other people's goods."[6] In an opinion mistakenly attributed to Julius Caesar, Machiavelli claims that "Caesar said that initially the French are more than men, but in the end they are less than women."[7] His opinion of the French was never favorable, especially since he resented Florence's dependency upon French arms as he later showed in *The Prince* (ch. 3) in reporting a famous retort to the French minister, Cardinal d'Amboise, who had criticized Italian military ability: "the Cardinal of Rouen telling me that the Italians had no comprehension of war, I answered that the French had no understanding of politics."[8] The disdain for the French shown in this often quoted passage from *The Prince* is anticipated in the short essay, *On the French National Character* (1503). This is a collection of thirteen maxim-like statements about the French people, and there is not a single compli-mentary remark in it. These epigrammatic judgments seem to be generalizations based upon Machiavelli's observations of the French monarch, Louis XII. For example, the statement that Louis only thought of "present convenience" in the dispatches becomes extended to the whole nation: "they think so much of the present advantage that they remember only vaguely past injuries or benefits and take little heed of the future, whether it be good or bad." [9] Two other terse comments recall Machiavelli's early words about the king's avarice: "they are more eager for money than for blood," and "they are liberal only in granting audiences." [10] Machiavelli's most damning comment is that the French disregard his beloved Romans: "they are enemies of the Roman language and of their fame." [11]

This attention to the "nature" of a historical character or of a nation reflects one aspect of the minor works, but it is the least important tendency in them that shaped the evolution of Machiavelli's art of portraiture. Such observations examined herein were only observations or opinions expressed in an aphoristic style without the detail to particulars that must characterize any great literature. Machiavelli would have to combine his ability to analyze the nature of historical figures with a more sophisticated theoretical framework and an increased attention to style before his character sketches would become a central aspect of his works. This is precisely what occurs in three short works written in 1503: *Remarks on the Raising of Money*; *On the Method of Dealing with the Rebellious Peoples of the Valdichiana*; and *A Description of the Method Used by Duke Valentino in Killing Vitellozzo Vitelli, Oliverotto da Fermo, and Others.*[12] In these works, Machiavelli avoids the kind of abstract evaluations of persons or nations which occurred in his diplomatic reports or in the minor works that dealt with his experiences in Germany or France.

Although there is some disagreement, most scholars believe that the *Remarks on the Raising of Money* is a speech never intended to be delivered, a work of Machiavelli's imagination or a *ghiribizzo*, to use Machiavelli's own word for such an expression of his fantasy.[13] Besides its intrinsic importance, it thus bears at least an indirect relationship to the imaginary speeches which are an integral part of character sketches in such later works as *The History of Florence* and *The Life of Castruccio Castracani of Lucca.* The work begins *in medias res* with the discussion of a theoretical problem, the implications of *forza* and *prudenza*, two qualities which for Machiavelli were "the two nerves of all governments that have existed or ever will exist in the world." [14] To clarify his discussion, he uses historical characters as exempla. History is implicitly seen as a vast didactic process, a source of information for the knowing observer. To show the Florentine rulers (the audience for this imaginary argument) the stupidity of their refusal to spend the necessary monies for the defense of their liberty, Machiavelli relates an anecdote about the emperor of Constantinople who tried for years to get his citizens to spend enough money to defend themselves from the Turks. Like the Florentines, his citizens become generous only when the enemy is at their gates:

As they heard the sounds of the artillery at their walls and the resounding noises of the enemy army, they ran in tears to the emperor with their aprons full of money. He chased them away from him, saying to them: "Go and die with this money, since you did not wish to live without it!" [15]

From this historical lesson, Machiavelli then turns to his own day, revealing his new historical method: "But it is not necessary for me to go to Greece for exempla, since I have them in Florence." [16] He then shows how the Florentine citizenry acted like their Byzantine counterparts when Cesare Borgia threatened their city. Though no character sketch of Borgia is presented in the work, the use of historical figures as exempla to bolster a theoretical argument will reappear in the other two important minor works as well as in all of Machiavelli's great treatises.[17]

The same kind of development can be observed in *A Description of the Method Used by Duke Valentino in Killing Vitellozzo Vitelli, Oliverotto da Fermo, and Others*. Here Machiavelli uses his own observations of Borgia at Imola, but he creates a purely literary work from them, modifying the facts as he had previously reported them in his letters to increase the impact his narrative would have upon his readers.[18] The work has such a dramatic quality that its five major episodes seem to be acts in an historical drama skillfully organized to create the maximum of "dramatic" tension. The opening lines describe the birth of the Magione conspiracy among his trusted lieutenants: "they felt that the duke was getting too powerful and that it was to be feared that, Bologna being occupied, he might try to destroy them in order to be the only armed man in Italy." [19] The second "act" relates the immediate results of the conspiracy — Urbino takes advantage of Borgia's momentary weakness and revolts against his rule. The story becomes most interesting in the third episode, for Machiavelli now begins to distort historical facts for his own literary purposes. Florence, he says, refused to aid the conspirators because of the hatred the city had for Vitellozzo Vitelli:

But the Florentines, because of the hatred they had for the Vitelli and the Orsini for several reasons, not only did not join the conspirators but sent Niccolò Machiavelli, their secretary, to offer the Duke aid and asylum against his new enemies. The Duke was then at Imola and was greatly afraid, since war was eminent and he was unarmed, for his soldiers had suddenly and without him knowing anything about it become hostile toward him.[20]

It is well to remember that in his original dispatches from Imola, Machiavelli had described Borgia as "a daring and fortunate man, full of hope"; there was never the least hint of Borgia being "greatly afraid" or "disarmed." An even more obvious alteration is the assertion that Machiavelli was sent to Imola to offer Borgia "aid and asylum against his new enemies." It is clear from the dispatches and from Machiavelli's instructions that he was under orders not to offer either side any aid until Florence could align herself with the victor.[21] Aid to Borgia was never even considered. After this initial distortion, Machiavelli then says that Borgia, "having regained his courage because of the offer of the Florentines, decided to gain time with the few soldiers he had and with peace negotiations." [22] Further increasing this second "correction" to his earlier account, Machiavelli injects himself into the story; it is almost as if he were claiming some of the credit for Borgia's later triumph by underlining the fact that he himself brought the aid that caused Borgia to regain his courage in the midst of impending disaster. Such a falsification motivated by Machiavelli's desire to link his own actions with those of Borgia is not without precedent in his life.[23]

The fourth part of the narrative relates Borgia's own reactions to the Magione conspiracy after having regained his courage. An initial military venture meets with failure. Since the tactics of the lion do not work, to use the metaphor of *The Prince* (ch. 18), Borgia then turns to the tactics of the fox:

and being a very great dissembler, he spared no effort to make them believe they had moved their forces against a man who intended what he had acquired to be theirs, and that it was sufficient for him to have the name of prince, but that he intended the principality to be their own.[24]

Though Borgia has assembled by this time an army superior to that of his enemies, his nature as a "very great dissembler" prevails, and he decides to destroy his opponents by deceit: "although he now found himself so strong that he could revenge himself in open warfare against his enemies, nevertheless he thought that deceiving them would be a more useful and secure method, and thus he did not stop the negotiations." [25] The two descriptions of Borgia, first as "greatly afraid" and then as "a very great dissembler" are designed to make the story of Borgia's triumph more dramatic. The first distortion makes his final success even more impressive, for unlike his later disgrace in Rome in his struggle for power with Pope Julius II, Borgia's courage and resourcefulness are never lessened by dire threats to his power. The danger Borgia incurs because of the Magione conspiracy only serves to underscore his cunning and resourcefulness when he finally destroys his enemies by treachery at Sinigaglia. Between the fourth part of the story and the final description of the events at Sinigaglia, the denouement of this historical drama, Machiavelli inserts a long description of the area around Sinigaglia. Such geographical landscapes are rarely shown in his works, but this idyllic interlude has a literary function. The contrast between the beautiful setting of the supposedly peaceful meeting between Borgia and his lieutenants and the cruel treachery that occurs there, the transformation of a *locus amoenus* into a place of violence, emphasizes the horrible nature of Borgia's deed.

The final act of the drama details the capture and execution of the conspirators. The passage from the dispatches depicting Vitellozzo's arrival into the trap is partially repeated:

And Vitellozzo, unarmed, in a cloak lined with green, looked very discouraged as though he was aware of his imminent death, and he caused (knowing the courage of the man and his past fortune) some amazement. And it is said that when he left his men to come to Sinigaglia to meet the duke, he acted as if it were his last departure from them; and he asked his lieutenants to give aid to his house and to its fortune, and he admonished his nephews to bear in mind the virtue of their fathers and uncles rather than the fortune of their house.[26]

Although each of the conspirators, including Vitellozzo, is strangled, and the Magione conspiracy is crushed, the elegiac tone of the description of Vitellozzo shows the man to be a worthy opponent and makes him look even more admirable than Borgia. Although Machiavelli is usually implacable in his attitude toward a man whose defeat is brought about by his own carelessness, he shows more pity for this defeated captain than he had for Borgia when his model prince was destroyed by the even more crafty Pope Julius II. Sasso claims that A Description of the Method Used by Duke Valentino in Killing Vitellozzo Vitelli, Oliverotto da Fermo, and Others ends by sacrificing interpretation to narrative, evaluation to description, but such a judgment ignores the literary impulse which caused Machiavelli to create and refashion the story from his earlier account in his diplomatic dispatches.[27] This work reports the events at Sinigaglia not as they were seen piecemeal by a young diplomat but as they were reorganized into a complex and dramatic narrative by a developing literary genius. The narrator presents Borgia as a living exemplum of cunning and courage. Here, as in the dispatches, his innermost qualities are represented through a narration of his actions. But Machiavelli now presents Borgia's actions at Sinigaglia within a structured work of art, and the result is an engaging literary portrait of a great military leader. For the first time in any of Machiavelli's works, a true hero has emerged, a protagonist in the literal sense of the word — one who shapes the course of events to his own purposes.

The final minor work that we shall examine, On the Method of Dealing with the Rebellious Peoples of the Valdichiana, represents the culmination of several trends already examined in other essays and is the work closest in spirit to both The Prince and the Discourses. The essay begins not with a consideration of the revolt against Florence but with Livy's story of how Rome acted in a similar situation. The idea that history provides a source of information and exemplary models is best expressed here long before it was presented in a more systematic form in either The Prince or the Discourses. Not only does Machiavelli refer modern practice to that of the ancients in this work as he so often does in the great political treatises, but he also mixes classical illustrations with those from his own day. Here again, Machiavelli's fascination with the figure of Cesare Borgia causes him to present the man's actions as models. Borgia attempted to build a state in Tuscany with little dependence upon foreign alliances, the value of which policy Machiavelli believes Florence has yet to learn:

Whoever has observed Cesare Borgia, called Duke Valentino, sees that in maintaining the states that he possesses, he never has intended to found his power upon Italian friendships, having always valued the Venetians very little and you [i.e., Florence] less. If this is true, it is because he plans to build himself so great a state in Italy that it will make him safe by himself, and that it will make his friendship desirable to any other power. . . . it remains to be seen if the times are suitable to give form to these designs of his.[28]

An analysis of Machiavelli's minor works shows that the early focus upon the "nature of the man" in the dispatches has been broadened, in some important instances, by Machiavelli's new view of history. Since Machiavelli wrote the dispatches during the same time that he produced the minor works, it is obvious that he did not develop his view of history apart from these early political experiences. Rather, he must have found it impossible in a medium such as a dispatch to discourse upon such theoretical matters and must have turned to these short essays to work out the implications of the observations he records in his letters. In the minor works, at least one essay, *Remarks on the Raising of Money*, is an imaginary speech, which presents one of the author's ideas in a form that makes its presentation more dramatic and less obviously colored by his own bias. This is a stylistic technique that will become increasingly important in the later historical works. More importantly, Machiavelli now clearly has a philosophy of history, best expressed in *On the Method of Dealing with the Rebellious Peoples of the Valdichiana*. History is viewed as a guide to modern practice, and

Machiavelli has already begun using the deeds and personalities of great men as exempla. Finally, and most importantly, Machiavelli has shown in *A Description of the Method Used by Duke Valentino in Killing Vitellozzo Vitelli, Oliverotto da Fermo, and Others* that he can combine a strictly literary presentation of historical data with his own theoretical purposes. In this essay, he has blended his view of history as a source of didactic information with an imaginative literary study of Cesare Borgia, changing or distorting historical facts he had himself witnessed whenever necessary to sketch Borgia's character more dynamically. Borgia thus emerges as a living exemplum of cunning and treachery, the leader who knows the ways of both the lion and the fox. In these early works, Machiavelli has learned a lesson that he will not forget in writing *The Prince* and the *Discourses*; he has discovered that the presentation of historical figures as exempla of his theoretical ideas makes his arguments much more persuasive.[29]

IV   *Symbolic Characters as Exempla in* The Prince *and the* Discourses

The most famous works by Machiavelli, *The Prince* and the *Discourses*, contain several kinds of exempla. One type is the simple naming of a character or situation, as in Machiavelli's definition of the kinds of recent principalities in *The Prince* (ch. 1): "The newly established ones are either completely new, as was Milan to Francesco Sforza, or else they are like members joined on to the hereditary state of the prince who acquires them, as is the kingdom of Naples for the King of Spain." [1] A second type is more elaborate, with explanatory material added to the simple evocation of a name: "We have, as an exemplum, the Duke of Ferrara, who was able to withstand the assaults of the Venetians in 1484 and of Pope Julius II in 1510, for no other reason than because of the long duration of his family's reign in that city." [2] Here, the illustrative example is more than a name, for it functions as a kind of proof of a more general theory — that it is far easier to maintain hereditary states than to maintain new ones. As important as these types of illustrations are to Machiavelli's works, they remain too abstract and too simple to contribute to his art of portraiture. It is a more complicated kind of exemplum, that wherein the application of a general concept is embodied in the words or deeds or even the personality of a great man, which contributed most directly to the art of Machiavelli's political treatises in both *The Prince* (1513) and the *Discourses* (1513–1519). [3]

Machiavelli's early diplomatic experience and his readings of the classics combined in these two treatises to produce the most systematic presentation of his revolutionary political philosophy. The theory of history that appears in the minor works is now broadened, and historical individuals are cited as models of correct political behavior, as evidence to support Machiavelli's general theories. His view that political activity is calculable and capable of imitation is based upon the assumption that men are always the same and that history, therefore, is a dependable guide. In the dedication of *The Prince,* Machiavelli defines the subject of the work as "the knowledge of the deeds of great men which I have learned through a long experience of modern events and a continuous study of the past." [4] In like manner, Machiavelli asserts that the topic of book 3 of the *Discourses* is "to show how the actions of some particular men made Rome great and produced in that city many good effects" (bk. 3, ch. 1).[5] The doctrine of imitation is an essential hypothesis in both works. In *The Prince,* using a metaphor also found in *The Book of the Courtier* by Castiglione,[6] Machiavelli says:

No one should be surprised if, in my discussion of dominions that are totally new both as to their prince and their composition, I bring forth the most striking exempla; because men almost always walk the paths made by others and procede in their actions by imitation, although they are not completely able to stay on the path of others nor attain the excellence of those they imitate, a prudent man should always follow the way taken by great men and imitate those who have been most outstanding; so that, if he does not match their greatness, at least his actions will have the smell of it; and he should act like those prudent archers who, when the place they wish to hit seems too far off, knowing the power of their bow, set their aim higher than the desired target, not in order to reach such a height with their arrow but rather to be able with such a high aim to hit their own target [ch. 6].[7]

In another memorable simile from the *Discourses,* Machiavelli compares the admiration of his day for classical art and the disregard for the example set by the actions of Greeks and Romans:

When we consider therefore how much honor is attributed to antiquity, and how many times, leaving aside infinite other examples, a fragment of an ancient statue has been bought at a great price, which we are desirous to possess to ornament our houses, or to give to artists who try to imitate them in their own works with great industry; and when we see, on the other hand, the powerful examples which history shows us that have been accomplished by ancient kingdoms and republics, by kings, captains, citizens, and legislators who have exhausted themselves for their fatherland that have been more often admired than imitated, or so much ignored that not the slightest trace of this ancient virtue remains, I cannot but be at the same time both amazed and sorry [bk. 1, preface].[8]

These quotations show that Machiavelli considered the actions of these "most striking exempla" to be essential to his arguments; they are not simply illustrations of his ideas but are themselves the source of his inspiration.

The Prince and the *Discourses* are neither biographical works nor studies in depth of famous historical characters; they are theoretical treatises which argue abstract ideas by examining the actions and personalities of great men. There is a great attention to rhetoric or persuasion in both works, for each character examined in depth serves as the basis of an argument. Machiavelli's purpose here is not the writing of history, but instruction. Consider, for instance, his treatment of King Louis XII in chapter 3 of *The Prince*. Machiavelli had earlier discussed this monarch's personality in the diplomatic dispatches, where he was pictured as an avaricious, shortsighted ruler who had little grasp of political realities. His personality was there presented abstractly, without close attention to his deeds. Here, in contrast, Louis's weakness is seen through a different perspective — his nature is viewed through his actions, and they in turn reflect his character. This is the manner in which Machiavelli treats his subjects in these theoretical works, and actions reveal the underlying character of the historical figures examined. The man is used as an exemplum to avoid, for "he did the opposite of those things that one must do in order to keep possession of a foreign state." [9] Though he quickly captured Lombardy with the aid of the Venetians and made Florence, Genoa, and other small cities client states, he made his first mistake in enlisting the aid of a natural enemy, Pope Alexander VI, to gain Romagna, thus increasing the church's power. He then added error to error:

And having made the first mistake, he was compelled to follow it up, so that in order to stop the ambition of Alexander and to prevent him from becoming the ruler of Tuscany, he was forced to come to Italy. And not happy with increasing the power of the church and losing his friends, because of his desire for the kingdom of Naples, he divided it with the king of Spain; and where he was first the arbiter of Italy, he now had a companion, so that the ambitious of that province who were dissatisfied with him might have someone else to appeal to.[10]

Louis illustrates magnificently how one political blunder leads to another, for he should have supported his allies to maintain his power in Italy. Instead, his shortsightedness makes him do the contrary. He lost Lombardy by not observing any of the "rules" followed by those in the past who had occupied foreign territory, and Machiavelli catalogs the six instances of his political blundering. Louis's example provides instruction, for his failure was "no miracle, but very natural and reasonable." [11] The result of Machiavelli's consideration of Louis's actions leads to "a general rule, which never or rarely fails: that whoever is the cause of another's becoming powerful is himself ruined." [12] Louis's character, now seen dynamically through his deeds instead of being evaluated in general terms as in the dispatches, is disastrous to his political goals. The six mistakes made by the ruler reflect his weak personality. Each is judged by the narrator, who guides the reader to agree with his own evaluation of the king.

Machiavelli's analysis of Cesare Borgia in *The Prince* is set within a discussion of *virtù* and *fortuna*. Here, he adapts his earlier analyses of the nature of this man to a new theoretical argument. The Sinigaglia episode, the nucleus of a short essay and the Imola dispatches, remains a key element in the portrayal of Borgia in *The Prince*. In *A Description of the Method Used by Duke Valentino in Killing Vitellozzo Vitelli, Oliverotto da Fermo, and Others*, Machiavelli had written a dramatic story which treated Borgia only implicitly as an exemplum. The storyteller simply narrated the "facts" he selected, seldom injecting himself into the account to comment on the significance of the events being described. In contrast, the narrator of *The Prince* constantly employs the device of direct address. The contrast between the long, detailed account of the Sinigaglia treachery in the earlier work and the report of the same event in *The Prince* is a result of Machiavelli's new point of view. Borgia is now explicitly an exemplum, a part of a larger argument: "I know of no better precepts to give a new prince than the example of his actions" (ch. 7).[13] Machiavelli has shifted the focus of the story from the action itself to the action as symbolic of Borgia's character. The Sinigaglia episode, brilliantly set within a literary framework in the earlier essay, is now reported quickly and without detail:

Borgia turned to deceit; and he knew how to disguise his aims so well that the Orsini, represented by Signor Paolo, made peace with him; and the duke did not fail to use every kind of courtesy in order to beguile Paolo, giving him money, robes, and horses; so that the simple-mindedness of the Orsini led them to Sinigaglia into his hands. Having finished off these leaders, and having reduced their followers to his friends, the duke had laid a very good foundation to his power.[14]

The discussion of Borgia's actions is a case study bearing out the truth of a theory, and Machiavelli's style changes accordingly. He eliminates details and adds more specifically rhetorical passages to the narrative so that the reader does not miss the points the master is trying to convey. Phrases such as "And, as this part is worthy of note and of being imitated by others, I do not want to omit it," or "But to return to where we left off" underline this new argumentative aspect of Borgia's character and exploits.[15]

Machiavelli's willingness to sacrifice historical details to his larger design often gives his examples in *The Prince* and the *Discourses* a schematic quality.[16] Especially in *The Prince*, there is little room in his argument from general problem to exemplum to general rule for extended treatment of the many particulars of a man's life that might reveal diverse or even conflicting personality traits. Here, only the cleverness of Borgia or the shortsightedness of Louis is revealed through their deeds; other aspects of the two men are ignored. In such exempla, therefore, there is little psychological depth, for the figure presented is not intended to display complex human motivations of a mental or moral nature. He is meant to be a vivid illustration of one central human trait which is pertinent to a problem at hand. Machiavelli's *virtù* (like Homer's *areté*) is a public, visible, and external quality.[17] In his narrative, Machiavelli examines public personality traits, those qualities (cleverness, bravery, cowardice, ambition, and the like) which can be easily illustrated through the analysis of a man's actions and which can be imitated or avoided. The description of Borgia's deeds at Sinigaglia in A *Description of the Method Used by Duke Valentino in Killing Vitellozzo Vitelli, Oliverotto da Fermo, and Others* is a more highly wrought work of art, but the figure of Cesare Borgia in *The Prince* also has the spark of life that only genuine literary characters possess. Specific historical detail is often eliminated to sharpen the argument, but Machiavelli's presentation of this terrible warrior and of other exempla never makes these figures hollow abstractions or blatant allegory.

One of Machiavelli's most famous images in *The Prince* is that of the lion and the fox, the twin aspects of force that must be joined to the prince's understanding of law, the human element of politics: "It is therefore necessary to be a fox to recognize the traps, and a lion to frighten the wolves" (ch. 18).[18] To illustrate this general precept, Machiavelli discusses the Roman Emperor Severus, a man even more successful than Cesare Borgia in combining the two methods of open force and hidden deceit. Machiavelli's rhetorical opening is a general question — how is an emperor to hold power when he must contend with two opposing parties, the army and the people? He then moves to the exemplum of Severus:

Because Severus possessed so much *virtù* that, maintaining the soldiers as friends even while he oppressed the people, he was always able to reign happily; for those traits of his made him, in the eyes of the soldiers and the people, so admirable that the former were amazed and stunned, and the latter were respectful and satisfied. And since the actions of this man were outstanding in a new prince, I want to briefly show how well he knew how to use the characteristics of the lion and the fox; whose natures, as I say above, it is necessary for a prince to emulate [ch. 19].[19]

Machiavelli then shows how cleverly Severus used the tactics of the lion and of the fox to gain and hold power. He alone, of a long line of rulers, managed to die a peaceful death after having destroyed one emperor (Julianus) and two rival claimants to power (Pescennius Niger and Albinus) by either force or guile, playing his enemies off against one another until they destroyed themselves. After his exposition of Severus's remarkable deeds, the narrator assumes a magisterial tone in a summary conclusion: "Whoever examines in detail, therefore, the actions of this man, will find him a very ferocious lion and an extremely astute fox . . . and will not be surprised that he, a new ruler, should have been able to hold so much power (ch. 19)."[20]

The exempla of Cesare Borgia, Louis XII, and Severus in *The Prince* all isolate and illustrate a single dominant character trait of an individual. From the description of their deeds, illustrating their personalities dynamically, Machiavelli then moves to a general rule "deduced" from their life histories. It is important to note that Machiavelli does not work empirically in the modern statistical manner; he does not deduce his general rules after examining a significant number of cases. Instead, he works upon the reader's imagination by citing a few vivid examples from history, the "deeds of great men," which are far more persuasive. His brief character sketches, portraits of a man's basic traits as seen through his actions, serve in place of strictly logical arguments. As Joseph A. Mazzeo has put it, Machiavelli has a "literary intelligence"; "aware that life escapes all the abstract schemes we may construct to control it . . . he teaches like an artist, by concrete examples to be applied to specific and typical situations." [21] Without these historical figures whose actions incarnate specific human attributes that Machiavelli wishes to define to form his general rules, his arguments would reveal themselves to be what they really are, nonscientific assertions or hypotheses rather than accepted historical verities, the status Machiavelli hoped to attain for them through his skillful rhetoric.

Besides citing the specific historical exempla Machiavelli uses to support his arguments, it is also possible to argue that another character sketch in *The Prince*, the picture of the ideal prince himself, is the sum total of the qualities portrayed in the separate episodes. Read in this way, the work would, to borrow a phrase from Castiglione, "form with words" the perfect prince instead of the perfect courtier.[22] This possibility has been mentioned by several critics, especially in relation to the important chapters 15 through 28.[23] These chapters, taken as a unit, are the most controversial parts of the work, and they give the reader a general outline of the new prince's moral characteristics. No actual historical figure has ever measured up to Machiavelli's standards; the ideal ruler would have the qualities of the politicians in these chapters. He should know how not to be good ("imparare a potere essere non buono," ch. 15) if that should become necessary; he should prefer to be called a miser if it will enable him to remain in power (ch. 16); when he must choose whether to be loved or feared, he should prefer to be feared, since men love at their own pleasure but fear at their prince's (ch. 17); he should appear to be "all mercy, all faith, all integrity, all humanity, all religion" without necessarily being so, since "men generally judge more by the eyes than by their hands; all are able to see, only a few to touch" (ch. 18).[24] Taken as a unit, these chapters discuss the nature of the new prince in much the same fashion as Machiavelli examined "the nature of the man" in his early letters and minor works. However, it would be a mistake to see this brief, abstract outline of moral qualities as the most important character sketch in the work. Machiavelli's style is slowly evolving towards a more descriptive art of portraiture with his use of historical exempla as symbolic characters. These model rulers (Borgia, Severus, Pope Julius, and many others) are the characters of *The Prince* that most readers and critics remember. As Machiavelli said in his dedicatory preface to Lorenzo de' Medici, his gift was not the portrait of the ideal prince but "the knowledge of the deeds of great men."

Giorgio Bàrberi Squarotti has taken this theory of a collective description of a single hero in the work even further, declaring that the form of the treatise is itself "tragic" in the Aristotelian sense, and that each important exemplum in the work is characterized by a tragic flaw caused by "opposizione delle cose" to the hero's designs.[25] This tempting thesis is undermined by the fact that Machiavelli's view of man was not a tragic one. In spite of all the evidence to the contrary (much of which he himself amassed in his own exempla), Machiavelli continued to believe in at least the possibility of human improvement, even if that improvement was a return to the past. J. H. Whitfield has persuasively argued that Machiavelli was an incurable optimist, especially if he is compared to the more realistic (and less imaginative) Guicciardini:

It is not pessimism to see things as wrong or bad, if they are wrong or bad. That is only accuracy of vision . . . and even if Machiavelli is not equal to the task [of providing solutions], he hopes to bring it near enough to completion for a successor to finish it. That is pure optimism; and it does not need the cautious Guicciardini to remind us how rash it was as optimism.[26]

Moreover, all of Machiavelli's exempla cannot be said to have been defeated by the same "malignity of fortune" that brought Cesare Borgia down. Severus is only one of many successful rulers who never seemed to evince such a tragic flaw.

In keeping with Machiavelli's didactic purpose in *The Prince*, his historical illustrations function rhetorically as a means of persuading his audience that his theories actually have the status of historical fact, usually forming the middle part of an argument that ranges from general problem to exemplum to general rule. Although the exempla are rarely psychologically complicated, and we seldom see more than one dominant trait of their personalities (the result of an understandable emphasis upon "public" qualities which could be imitated or avoided by his readers), Machiavelli never makes his historical protagonists mere footnotes to his arguments. No critic would claim that Borgia, for instance, "stands for" or "signifies" Cunning or Deceit in the same manner that such an allegorical poet as Spenser would use Red Cross or Una in *The Faerie Queene* as a "type" of Christ, Holiness, or the Church. Machiavelli's characters are "natural symbols" or "symbolic personnages," to borrow terms from Dorothy Sayers's description of Dantean figures, for his exempla have both a literal meaning (that is, the narrative is intended to relate a true story) and a symbolic significance, since the character presented becomes emblematic of a particular personality and the political consequences of such a personality in action.[27]

The exempla in the *Discourses* differ in several respects from those in *The Prince*. In the first place, Machiavelli is freer to expand his treatments of historical figures because the treatise is supposed to be a commentary on an historical work. Such men also tend to reappear in this larger work. For example, Piero Soderini is discussed several times (bk. 3, chs. 3, 9, 30), each time in a different context, but in each instance, the reference underlines how his humanity, kindness, and lack of ability to change his nature when the times called for more drastic measures led to his undoing. In like manner, Julius Caesar appears many times (bk. 1, chs. 10, 17, 33, 37; bk. 3, ch. 6), in each instance exemplifying the prototype of a tyrant. As the reader of the *Discourses* notes the reappearance of these and other men, he begins to identify them with the personality traits that they and their actions represent, and the figure takes on the qualities of a symbolic personage.[28]

A good example of how this technique produced an outstanding episode in the *Discourses* is the description of the encounter of Pope Julius II and Gianpaolo Baglioni at Perugia (bk. 1, ch. 27). In every passage that mentions this warrior pope (bk. 1, ch. 27; bk. 2, ch. 29; bk. 3, chs. 9, 46), Julius is taken as the perfect illustration of the impetuous man who is always successful because the times called for rash deeds. This trait was identified with the pope as early as Machiavelli's Roman dispatches, where the pope even replaced Cesare Borgia in Machiavelli's esteem. The encounter of this impulsive man with the tyrant of Perugia is set within a discussion of the dangers of moderate courses of action: "But men choose certain middle courses which are most dangerous; for they know neither how to be entirely good nor entirely evil, as we shall demonstrate by examples in the next chapter" (bk. 1, ch. 26).[29] Again, Machiavelli distorts an earlier account of this same event which he had related in a dispatch to the Florentine Chancellery written on 13 September 1506. In that letter, Machiavelli told how the pope's impatient nature had led him to enter the city of Perugia almost alone and unarmed, even though his intention was to remove Gianpaolo from power. Although the tyrant had the chance to avenge himself upon the pope, he declined to do so:

Nevertheless, Julius and his cardinals are at the mercy of Gianpaolo and are not in control of the situation: and if Gianpaolo does not harm the man who has come to seize his state, it is probably because of his good nature and humanity . . . one time Gianpaolo said that he knew two ways to save his dominion; one with force, the other with humility, and in putting his trust in his friends that give him counsel: and he did not want to choose the first method, but turned to the second.[30]

Here, Gianpaolo is pictured as a perfect gentleman, a man of humanity who out of prudence rejects a drastic but necessary means of solving his dilemma. The initial picture of this encounter as it is reported in the dispatches lacks any dramatic qualities or any exemplary importance. In the *Discourses*, Machiavelli changes this earlier account, distorting his previous description to make the event more exciting and theoretically more significant. The pope's characteristic impetuosity leads him to enter the city undefended and unarmed: "And thus, with the usual furor with which he governed all his affairs, Julius placed himself in the hands of his enemy with only a small guard; nevertheless, he carried Gianpaolo off with him, leaving a governor in that city to act in the name of the Church" (bk. 1, ch. 27).[31] The event startled even the men who had accompanied Julius to Perugia, since they could not understand why Gianpaolo had surrendered:

The temerity of Julius and the cowardice of Gianpaolo were noted by prudent men who were with the pope; nor could they understand why Gianpaolo had not by a single blow rid himself of his enemy, whereby he would have gained for himself perpetual fame and rich spoils, since the pope was accompanied by all the cardinals with their valuable possessions [bk. 1, ch. 27].[32]

It is no longer Gianpaolo's good nature or his humanity that hinders him from taking advantage of his enemy's impetuous nature but paradoxically his cowardice — killing the prelate and his party would have given him an eternal reputation for valor. Adding details of Baglioni's life that had been ignored in the diplomatic letters, Machiavelli asserts that it was not because of Gianpaolo's goodness or scruples of conscience ("bontà o per conscienza") that he refrained from such a crime, for this had not kept him from keeping his sister as a mistress or from murdering his cousins and nephews. In such a vicious man (*uomo facinoroso*), there could never be any sentiment of respect. From this extraordinary encounter, Machiavelli then deduces the rule that "men do not know how to be honorably wicked or perfectly good, and when a crime has in itself some grandeur or magnanimity, they will not know how to perform it" (bk. 1, ch. 27).[33] Machiavelli would have preferred a splendid act of wickedness to this odious halfway measure on Baglioni's part:

Thus, Gianpaolo, who did not mind incest or public parricide, did not know how, or, to put it better, did not dare to attempt an act (having a justifiable opportunity) for which everyone would have admired his courage, and which would have gained for him eternal fame as being the first man to show these prelates how little esteem those who live and govern as they do merit, and as having done a deed whose greatness would have surpassed its infamy and every danger that could have resulted from it [bk. 1, ch. 27].[34]

One recent critic has called Machiavelli a "matchless ironist," [35] and no better example of Machiavelli's ironic diction could be found than the paragraph above. Such diction often borders on sarcasm and usually reflects Machiavelli's contempt for the man he is examining. We have already seen this stylistic feature of his works in the diplomatic letters, where Machiavelli's ironic language revealed his dislike for Louis XII or Maximilian of Germany by describing them as "prudent," "good," or "humane." In each case, the modifiers actually connoted derogatory evaluations of the two rulers. Far from being prudent, Louis was stupidly unimaginative; the goodness or humanity of the German ruler was actually credulity. In his treatment of Gianpaolo, the same penchant for irony is evident and is developed at length. The fact that the tyrant of Perugia failed to commit a brutal murder is not praised but is instead called cowardice (*viltà*). Ironically, Gianpaolo has lost "eternal fame" by his restraint. Machiavelli's dislike for Gianpaolo becomes even more obvious as he injects a parenthetical phrase into the narrative after the verb "did not know how" to explain what he really means — "or, to put it better, did not dare." The tyrant thus knew how to be evil (as his incest or his other murders indicated), but he dared not commit a truly grand crime. Machiavelli's sarcasm continues as phrase after phrase is skillfully employed by the narrator in an indictment of Gianpaolo. Those critics who wish to see in Machiavelli a complete separation of politics and morality could find no better argument than the diction of this episode, for Machiavelli repeatedly reverses the conventional morality by praising infamy (when employed in a grand manner) and damning moderation or Christian restraint as a greater political blunder than murder.[36] In a manner akin to the heroes of Corneille's theater, Machiavelli's heroes are those whose actions produce *ammirazione* — a term which is "closer to a kind of wonder, of amazement" [37] than it is to moral approval. Thus, in spite of his stupidity in entering what should have been a perfect trap, Pope Julius emerges from this encounter as the hero while Gianpaolo is the villain because he fails to take advantage of his opportunity. By altering the "facts" of his earlier account to match his new purpose, Machiavelli has turned an historical event into a living illustration of the confrontation between two archetypal personalities. From history he has created a dramatic scenario.

Machiavelli's admiration for characters whose personalities and actions incarnate exemplary traits led him to cite many events of doubtful historical importance but which clearly reflected the character traits necessary for great political leaders. One of the most interesting illustrations of courage in the *Discourses* occurs in a chapter dealing with conspiracies.[38] Conspirators in the town of Forlì had killed the ruler, Count Girolamo, and had captured his wife and children, leaving only a fortress still held by soldiers loyal to the count's family. Since the master of the fortress was unwilling to yield, the Countess Caterina persuaded her captors that she could arrange for a surrender while the plotters kept her children as hostages, and so they permitted her to enter the castle. Once safely inside the fortress, the woman refused to honor her agreement, and her actions appealed to Machiavelli's sense of grandeur:

As soon as she was inside, she reproached them for the murder of her husband and threatened them with every kind of vendetta. And to prove to them that she cared little for her children, she showed them her genital parts, saying that she still had the means of producing more of them. Thus the conspirators, without counsel and having recognized only too late their mistake, suffered the penalty of their imprudence with a perpetual exile [bk. 3, ch. 6].[39]

Not a word in this brief vignette discusses the fate of her children; only her remarkable gesture on the fortress walls (and the bravery it reflected in the lady's character) interests Machiavelli. The Countess Caterina embodies here the very essence of personal courage, just as Gianpaolo incarnated mediocrity in evil-doing and Pope Julius represented impetuousness. Although the fate of her children is not mentioned, the implication is clear that the gesture of the woman so disconcerted the conspirators that they gave up their scheme to capture Forlì and retired in disgrace.

Machiavelli often studies the actions of an historical character in great detail in the *Discourses*, as in his extended treatment of Appius Claudius. In many ways, this episode foreshadows the portrait of the Duke of Athens in *The History of Florence,* one of the most complex character sketches in all of Machiavelli's works. Like the Duke of Athens, Appius Claudius is a man who uses his hypocrisy to conceal his true motives until he has seized power; like the duke, his own nature contains the seeds of both his rise to power and his downfall. Appius is initially described as a "shrewd and restless man" (bk. 1, ch. 40). After he is appointed to the decemvirate to rule Rome while new laws are devised, Appius's cunning, restless nature leads him to take advantage of his position to work for more power. Although he had long been known for his hatred of the common people, he begins to curry their favor to gain popular support against the other nine nobles of the ruling decemvirate: "for he had made himself so popular with his actions, that it seemed a miracle how he could so quickly have taken on a new nature and a new spirit, being considered until that time a cruel persecutor of the plebians" (bk. 1, ch. 40).[40] Given Machiavelli's feeling that people judge only by appearances ("Everyone sees what you appear to be, few feel what you are," *The Prince,* ch. 28), he often praises such hypocrisy (as in the cases of Borgia or Pope Julius) when it serves a higher political purpose.[41] Appius, like so many petty tyrants Machiavelli describes, is only interested in personal gain and lacks any of the compensating and laudable traits that made Borgia's treachery so exciting to Machiavelli. Machiavelli therefore disapproves of Appius, even though he finds that some of his techniques are exemplary. Appius's growing popularity with the commoners led the nobles to grow suspicious of their former ally. Fearing to act openly against him, they decide to let him suggest the next ten names for the decemvirate of the coming year, hoping that he will be forced to curb his ambition when called upon to make such an obvious show of his intentions. Though Appius has feigned magnanimity up to this time, he now decides to seize power with this unexpected opportunity: "In truth, he converted the impediment into an opportunity, and named himself as among the first to the amazement and displeasure of all the nobles: then he nominated nine others to suit his plans" (bk. 1, ch. 40).[42] The mask of hypocrisy, so successfully worn until this time to cloak his true motives, is now removed as Appius's nature drives him to feats of extraordinary arrogance, revealing his true nature even to the unsuspecting commoners:

For Appius quickly put an end to his feigned character and began to show his innate pride, and in a few days he tainted his colleagues with his own manners. And in order to intimidate the populace and the Senate, in place of the usual twelve lictors they employed one hundred and twenty [bk. 1, ch. 40].[43]

His arrogance leads him to increase the size of his bodyguard by ten times the legal number. His overbearing nature, for so long covered by his clever hypocrisy, seemed to have no bounds, for it led him to believe that he was above the law. As so often is the case, a relatively minor incident led to Appius's downfall by so arousing the city's moral indignation that he was forcefully removed from office:

Then it happened that he fell in love with Virginia, and that desiring her, he took her off by force so that her father Virginius killed her in order to free her; this provoked violent disturbances in Rome and in the armies: the soldiers and the people marched to the Mons Sacer, where they remained until the Decemvirs abdicated their power and the Consuls and the Tribunes were reestablished, and Rome was restored to the form of its ancient liberty [bk. 1, ch. 40].[44]

A comparison of Machiavelli's version of this story and the account that he found in Livy (bk. 3, chs. 38–58) reveals how Machiavelli modified Livy's interpretation of this event. Livy uses twenty-six chapters to examine the same material that Machiavelli condenses into one concise chapter by ignoring Livy's long, stylized speeches and the many details that the Latin historian included which were irrelevant to

Machiavelli's new purpose. Machiavelli concentrates only upon
the personality of Appius and how it was reflected in his actions, while Livy places Appius in a broader historical framework of a discussion of the class struggles in ancient Rome.
Livy was primarily interested in moral exempla, in the stories
from Roman history and legend which served to explain the
city's greatness. The center of the Latin account is not Appius
but is Virginius, who kills his own daughter to save her from
dishonor: "Permission being granted, he led his daughter and
the nurse apart, to the booths near the shrine of Cloacina, now
known as the 'New Booths,' and there, snatching a knife from
a butcher, he exclaimed, 'Thus, my daughter, in the only way
I can, do I assert your freedom!' " (bk. 3, ch. 43).[45] Like the
dishonor of Lucretia by the lustful Tarquinian tyrants of early
Rome which was avenged by Brutus and which resulted in the
original Roman Consulate (Livy, bk. 1, chs. 43–59), the crimes
of Appius against the family of Virginius are used by Livy to
set up the account of the abolition of the decemvirate and the
reestablishment of the older system of democratic government:
"The wildest excitement prevailed amongst the people, occa-
sioned in part by the atrocity of the crime [Appius's crime, not
Virginius's justifiable and exemplary murder to save his daughter's honor], in part by the hope of improving the opportunity
to regain their liberty" (bk. 3, ch. 44).[46] Livy's prime concern is
explaining how the example of Virginius's courage spurred the
Roman people to regain their lost liberty. In his history, the
actions of Appius are of secondary importance to the account
of Virginius's sacrifice. While Livy devotes fifteen chapters to
Appius's lust for Virginia, her subsequent murder, and the resulting political changes, Machiavelli mentions these events in
a single paragraph. The six Latin quotations he includes in his
own version (taken almost verbatim from Livy) may lead a
careless reader to conclude that Machiavelli is simply repeating
an episode from the Latin original, but the purpose of each
story is fundamentally different. The effect of the Latin quotations gives Machiavelli's version the status of a commentary,

but his changes are in fact substantial ones, and he shifts the focus of the tale away from the redemptive sacrifice of a daughter upon the altar of Roman virtue to an analysis of Appius's nature and how his character is revealed through his deeds. Machiavelli's rewriting of Livy is even clearer in the summary chapter which Machiavelli uses to evaluate the tyrant's actions. Appius's mistake was his sudden shift from one nature to another, from his false appearance to his true character: "Besides the other errors made by Appius in order to maintain his tyranny, that of changing too quickly from one quality to another was of no little import" (bk. 1, ch. 41).[47] Most of his deceits were admittedly cleverly executed, especially his hypocritical support of the populace against the nobility and his audacity in naming himself and nine of his cronies to the decemvirate. But his own wicked nature was not sufficiently strong to remain hidden behind his mask of deceit, and it was thus very ill advised to "suddenly change his nature — from being a friend of the people to showing himself an enemy, from being humane to becoming arrogant, from being easy to reach to becoming inaccessible — and to do this so quickly and without any excuse that everybody could see the falseness of his heart" (bk. 1, ch. 41).[48] Appius is unmasked by the very quality that enabled him to attain his success. When his true character is given free expression, his hypocrisy becomes so blatant that it is evident even to the gullible commoners.

Machiavelli's presentation of historical figures has evolved greatly since his initial attempts to sketch the "nature of the man" in his diplomatic dispatches. There, his observations were delivered randomly and served only to inform the Chancellery about the personalities of their allies or adversaries. Now, within his new theoretical framework of didactic history, Machiavelli's characters function as an integral part of a dynamic political theory. They are "symbolic personages" or "natural symbols," not just hollow abstractions, for their unique historical lives incarnate certain archetypal human characteristics — Countess Caterina becomes the perfect example of courage; Cesare Borgia represents the man of *virtù* who is defeated by *fortuna;* Gianpaolo Baglioni exemplifies the mediocre villain incapable of anything except petty crime. All of these characters, and countless others, animate Machiavelli's theoretical arguments. His political philosophy still interests the modern reader because it is so replete with the stuff that makes great literature — memorable characters whose particular actions or personalities embody universal dimensions of the human spirit. It is not just a coincidence that terms from Dantean criticism such as "symbolic personages" or "natural symbols" fit these figures, for the similarity between Dante's characters and Machiavelli's is a close one. Both men avoid simple allegory or personification of abstract qualities, preferring instead to present historical characters who have a literal significance as well as a symbolic dimension as representatives of certain universal human characteristics. Erich Auerbach has shown how Dante was the first modern European writer to assert that the individual human destiny was:

not meaningless, but that it is necessarily tragic and significant, and that the whole world context is revealed in it. . . . Modern mimesis found man in his individual destiny; it raised him out of the two-dimensional unreality of a remote dreamland or philosophical abstraction and moved him into the historical area in which he really lives.[49]

Machiavelli, like other Italian writers to follow Dante, abandons most of the religious concepts that were the foundation of Dante's historical view of man, but in spite of this modification, Dante's contribution to the representation of human reality remained essentially intact. As Joseph A. Mazzeo has noted, the concept of hell unites these two great Florentines, for "Machiavelli's analysis of experience is made entirely in terms of incontinence, force, and fraud, Dante's three categories of sin."[50] This examination of Machiavelli's natural symbols shows that the presentation of historical figures in *The Prince* and the *Discourses* embodies Dante's idea that the individual's actions are "significant" (though not necessarily "tragic") within a new political framework, for the actions of his characters reveal rules of political behavior that are assumed to be universally valid. The sketches of exempla incarnating universal human qualities are blended into a larger argument with great skill, so that these two treatises seem to furnish irrefutable historical proof of the hypotheses contained in each.

In addition to the use of "symbolic characters" in these two major works, they also show a shift in emphasis. In *The Prince*, the character sketches are necessarily brief because of the polemical nature of the work itself. In the *Discourses*, however, Machiavelli is freer to elaborate his descriptions, offering more details about a character or, as in the case of the Countess Caterina at Forlì, describing some striking anecdote from history which aroused his imagination. Although his emphasis is always upon the rhetorical implications of his exempla, it is evident in the transition from *The Prince* to the *Discourses* that he gives increasing attention to the literary aspects of his character presentation. Machiavelli's art of portraiture never becomes completely divorced from his theoretical concerns, but in the last major works, *The History of Florence* and *The Life of Castruccio Castracani of Lucca*, argument becomes a secondary consideration as the portraits themselves become the most important aspect of the works. In these last two writings, when Machiavelli adds color and supporting literary details to his already highly developed style in the presentation of historical figures, his portraits become truly literary creations, historical protagonists who exist in a literary universe and who no longer need theoretical arguments to justify their existence.

V

Castruccio Castracani: Machiavelli's Archetypal Prince

The Life of Castruccio Castracani of Lucca (1520) is Machiavelli's first attempt to study an historical character in depth, for the entire life of this thirteenth-century condottiere is examined. Unlike the often schematic portraits of his earlier works, this character sketch is both exemplum and historical myth. Machiavelli systematically reshapes the man's life to make it an archetypal presentation of the ideal prince. While the didactic intent of the work is clear, the focus of the narrative is not simply instruction, for this is a purely literary work, never intended to be an accurate biography. It has often been overlooked, however, because of the common (and understandable) critical preoccupation with Machiavelli's major theoretical works. When it is discussed at all, it is usually defined simply as an idealized biography, a preface to or a test-piece for *The History of Florence*.[1] Few critics grant this work the importance I believe it deserves or examine it in detail, primarily because the focus of their studies is usually historical rather than literary. The most important article on the biography even denies that it represents an idealization of Castruccio and proposes instead that Machiavelli actually condemns Castruccio as one of the "insolent men" of *The History of Florence* (bk. 4, ch. 1) — "not the legislator who begets *ordini* and stability, but the conqueror who blazes like a meteor, and then meets eclipse."[2] J. H. Whitfield would have us believe further that Machiavelli was "by temperament careless in points of detail," and that his insertions of fictional elements into this biography were unmotivated or, at least, unimportant since Machiavelli was no more inaccurate than other historians of his day.[3] I contend that Whitfield's analysis of this work errs, not only in its examination of the text but also in its assumptions about Renaissance history and biography. Contrary to his views, the adjustments and corrections Machiavelli makes in the narration of Castruccio's life are those which underline the exemplary qualities of the man and which make him a mythological figure, an archetypal prince. Far from being a "prentice-piece of historical narrative, a summer month's diversion," this work is the culmination of a stylistic tendency toward the presentation of character sketches which Machiavelli began to practice as early as his diplomatic dispatches and which he continued through all his works.[4]

The idealization of important historical protagonists is a trait of classical biography and history. Since history and rhetoric were seen as sister arts, the purpose of one (instruction) was furthered by the skillful literary (and therefore rhetorical) presentation of the major characters in the narrative. Scholes and Kellogg indicate that such historical biography is

almost the perfect complement of realistic fiction. Its subject is real, a "historical" personage, but its substance is highly fictionalized in the interest of emotion and moral instruction; to move and to teach is its object. . . . In an empirically oriented culture, biography will tend to develop in the direction of "scientific" accuracy of fact; but without continual pressure from empirical modes of thought, the Life quickly slides over into romance, as it did in the saint's-life formulations of the Middle Ages.[5]

Scholars of Renaissance humanist historiography, such as Felix Gilbert and Peter Burke, have demonstrated that the humanists were not adverse to stylizing and embellishing the event or the person about whom they were writing. Historical characters often assumed stereotyped forms just as painters followed classical models and poets imitated classical *topoi:*

what mattered to the Renaissance historian was not to convey any precise indication of the individuality of *this* man, or to describe precisely what was said or done on *this* occasion, but to give a general impression of *a* leader, *a* battle, *an* oration. If the evidence was not available, it was permissable . . . to invent.[6]

What is perhaps less obvious is that this trait of humanist historiography has important medieval as well as classical precedents.

E. H. Gombrich has noted that the medieval portrait was rarely an accurate copy of the person portrayed but was frequently a stereotyped idealization: "all the artist did was to draw a conventional figure and to give it the insignia of office — a crown and sceptre for the king, a mitre and crozier for the bishop." [7] This characteristic of medieval art had its counterpart in literature as well. Disputing Burckhardt's contention that hero worship began in the Renaissance, Johan Huizinga underlines the fact that the

aspiration to the splendour of antique life, which is the characteristic of the Renaissance, had its roots in the chivalrous ideal. . . . This hero-worship of the declining Middle Ages finds its literary expression in the biography of the perfect knight. In this genre the figures of recent history gradually superseded the legendary ones.[8]

Commenting on one such biography, that of a certain Marshal Boucicaut, Huizinga remarks that

the real facts of this hard life of a captain and statesman disappear beneath the appearances of ideal heroism. The marshal is depicted as the type of frugal and pious knight, at once courtly and well read. . . . The real Boucicaut did not altogether resemble this portrait; no one would have expected it.[9]

73

Other medieval examples of idealized and stylized portraiture have been found in the romances of Chrétien de Troyes[10] or in the *Cantar de mio Cid,* where Thomas R. Hart has demonstrated that the epic has both a literal or historical meaning (since it is in most respects a true story) and a figurative meaning (since the Cid is portrayed as an exemplary hero by the poet's rearrangements of historical events).[11]

Simple idealization of an historical protagonist would not, therefore, explain the originality of Machiavelli's biography, for he goes beyond this common practice and creates what must be termed an archetypal portrait of an ideal prince based upon a recognizable literary design that Jan De Vries has called the "pattern of an heroic life." [12] In the literary pattern of the heroic life, the hero often has a miraculous begetting and an obscure birth. There may be a threat to him in his youth. Romulus, Moses, and Oedipus, for example, were abandoned by their parents and were later found by shepherds or passersby. The hero reveals his particular qualities of courage and strength at an early age. There is usually an important battle to test his strength, a kind of rite of passage from youth to manhood, and the favor of a beautiful maiden is often his reward. A quest, even a trip to the underworld, is not uncommon. The last scene in the heroic life is the hero's death, an event which further reveals his exemplary ·qualities. As De Vries says, "naturally, not every heroic life shows the complete pattern," [13] and it is, moreover, not necessary that any hero reflect all these varied stages to follow the general design. As in any generic classification, there need be only a reasonable number of the "family resemblances" that are common to the generic group as a whole to apply the generic name to the specific case.[14]

Viewed from the literary perspective of this heroic-life pattern, Machiavelli's biography clearly is .both a literary work structured upon an archetypal framework and a political exemplum based upon historical fact. The work no longer is a moral exemplum at the service of the traditional Christian morality as were its medieval predecessors but now depicts the

principe nuovo, the practical man of *virtù*. The simple idealized biography described by Huizinga is now broadened by a
whole series of literary allusions as a result of the archetypal
framework. There is ample textual evidence to support this
interpretation, although it has not heretofore been advanced
in specific terms. The biography opens with a specific reference
to its archetypal nature. Machiavelli notes in his first paragraph
that most men who have accomplished great deeds had low or
obscure births and were exposed to beasts by their parents while
still babes; many were even adopted by the gods:

> To those who consider it, my dearest Zanobi and Luigi, it appears
> a wonderful thing that all those, or the majority of them, who
> have done very great deeds in this world, and who have been
> outstanding among the men of their day, have both in their origin
> and their birth been humble and obscure, or have been afflicted by
> fortune in an extraordinary manner; because all of them have been
> either exposed to wild animals or have had such base parents that,
> being ashamed of them, they have made themselves sons of
> Jupiter or some other god. Who these men are, since many of them
> are known to all, would be boring to repeat and little acceptable
> to the readers; therefore, we shall omit their names as superfluous.[15]

These heroes (left unnamed by Machiavelli because he assumed his readers would recognize them immediately) are
probably Moses and Romulus. If Marcello Virgilio Adriani
really had any influence upon Machiavelli's thinking, as has
been recently suggested, this passage may also refer to many
heroes of Homeric legend.[16]

Thus, Castruccio's entrance into the world must reflect the obscure birth and exposure that Moses and Romulus
experienced to fulfill the requisites of the heroic life, even if
such an event never actually occurred. "So, then, Castruccio
Castracani was one of those men," Machiavelli says, "and like
the others, he had neither a happy nor a renowned birth, as will
be clear in the narration of the course of his life." [17] Castruccio's
first appearance in the biography is thus a complete fabrica-

tion; he is discovered exposed in a vineyard by a priest and his sister:

It happened one morning just after sunrise, while Madonna Dianora (for that was Messer Antonio's sister's name) was walking through the vineyard picking, as is the custom of women, certain herbs for seasonings, that she heard a rustling under a vine in the thicket, and turning her glance there, she heard a weeping sound. She therefore moved toward the noise, and she uncovered through the foliage the hands and face of a baby boy who seemed to ask her for help. . . . Taking a nurse into the home, therefore, the brother and sister brought the baby up as if he were their own son; and when they baptized him, they named him Castruccio in memory of their father.[18]

After noting the affinities between this event and that of other legendary heroes, Machiavelli continues his creation of myth from history. As Joseph Campbell observes, "the makers of legend have seldom rested content to regard the world's great heroes as mere human beings who broke past the horizons that limited their fellows. . . . On the contrary, the tendency has always been to endow the hero with extraordinary powers from the moment of his birth." [19] Machiavelli felt this same impulse to make Castruccio's whole life amazing, even his childhood. Instead of studying for the priesthood as Antonio desired, Castruccio immediately began to lean toward a military life:

he laid his church books aside and began to occupy himself with arms; nor did he delight in anything save handling them or in running, jumping, wrestling, and other sports wherein he showed the greatest strength of mind and body, and far surpassed others of his age. If he ever did read, nothing pleased him except those accounts of wars or the deeds of the greatest men.[20]

His youthful prowess was noticed by a Ghibelline condottiere, Francesco Guinigi, who felt that Castruccio was destined to become a great military leader. To Guinigi, it seemed that besides surpassing the other young boys in the town, Castruccio had over them a kingly authority ("una autorità regia"), what a modern writer would call charisma.

The condottiere assumed the task of the youth's up-bringing, and under his tutelage, Castruccio's extraordinary development and his charismatic effect on his fellows con-tinued:

it is an extraordinary thing to consider in what a very short time he acquired all those abilities and habits that are required of a true gentleman. He first became an excellent horseman, riding even the wildest horse with skill; and in jousts and tournaments, although he was still quite young, he was more outstanding than others, so that in whatever feat of strength or skill, he found no man to surpass him.[21]

His physical strength and moral qualities soon made him the favorite not only of Lucca but of all Lombardy. Machiavelli then turns to the story of Castruccio's rise from obscurity to political power. At this point in other accounts of a hero's life, there are often battles with monsters, trips to the underworld, or damsels in distress. But Machiavelli was not interested in the kind of fantastic adventures we find in Ariosto's *Orlando furioso*. His interests, as always, are political ones, and it is only natural that the trials his hero has to undergo, the rites of passage from youth to fame, are political or military ones. After the death of his patron, Francesco Guinigi, Castruccio found an ally in the Ghibelline ruler of Pisa, Uguccione della Faggiuola d'Arezzo. Machiavelli moves from this historical fact to the fuller expression of his creative imagination, for the rest of the story is a product of his fantasy. The battle of Mon-tecatini (29 August 1315) was a splendid victory for Uguc-cione's forces over the exiled Guelfs of Lucca and their Floren-tine supporters, but Machiavelli distorts the historical facts to use the battle to enhance Castruccio's stature. He invents a reason for Uguccione's absence from the battle: "But as his illness grew more serious, Uguccione withdrew to Montecarlo for treatment, and left Castruccio in charge of the army." [22] Having removed the actual victor from the scene, Machiavelli then attributes the subsequent victory to Castruccio's genius. According to this rewritten version of the battle of Montecatini, Castruccio used a brilliant stratagem which resulted in the complete rout of his opponents; whereas he lost less than 300 men, the enemy suffered casualties of more than 10,000. The tremendous disparity in these figures is reminiscent of the battles of *La Chanson de Roland*. Here, as in the epic, casualty figures are complete fabrications, invented by Machiavelli to underscore his hero's amazing military victory. The tactical maneuver that wins the day in this imaginary battle is, as one might expect in Machiavelli, similar to a battle plan used by Scipio in Spain which he describes elsewhere in *The Art of War*.[23]

Having reshaped the story of Montecatini to this degree, Machiavelli is then able to incorporate Uguccione's resulting jealousy into the dramatic account of how Castruccio rose to power. Driven by envy of Castruccio's victory, Uguccione names his son Neri (instead of the more deserving Castruccio) as head of Lucca and then plans to seize and execute Castruccio during a banquet held in his honor. The plot fails, and Castruccio is freed by the city's citizens and becomes himself master of the city: "But Castruccio from a prisoner became like the prince of Lucca, and with the aid of his friends and the fresh favor of the people, he managed to be named captain of their army for a year." [24] "From a prisoner became like the prince of Lucca" — in this short phrase, Machiavelli concentrates all of his admiration for Castruccio's *virtù*. In a characteristic manner, Machiavelli expresses this sudden reversal of his hero's fortune with an emphasis upon the polar extremes of the situation, using the resulting contrast to achieve the maximum impact upon the reader's imagination.

Just as Machiavelli's perfect prince must combine the qualities of lion and fox, so Castruccio shows himself apt in the practice of both force and deceit. To demonstrate that Castruccio's victory at Montecatini was not mere chance, Machiavelli juggles the facts, combining the events of two earlier victories — Altopascio (23 September 1315) and Carmignano (14 May 1326) — into an imaginary battle that, once again, produces a brilliant victory and enormous enemy casualties. Castruccio's opponents lose 20,231 men while his own troops' loss is only a fraction of that number. Far from being "careless in points of detail," as Whitfield would have us believe, Machiavelli is meticulous in recasting small details to give his fictitious insertions an aura of historical veracity as he has done here in inventing precise casualty figures. Castruccio is thus the perfect lion, the master of the application of force.

But the ideal prince must also know how to deceive, and Machiavelli therefore reports two similar events which show Castruccio's ability to dissimulate. After a revolt against him in Lucca led by the Poggio family, Castruccio accepted the mediation of Stefano Poggio, a peaceful member of the family who had not taken part in the conspiracy, and he called the conspirators together in order, as he put it, to thank them for the opportunity of demonstrating his clemency and liberality. The gullible Poggio family accepted Castruccio's promised amnesty with the predictable result: "Having come, therefore, on the faith of Castruccio and Stefano, they were all imprisoned, and along with Stefano, they were executed." [25] In another instance, which he fabricated even to inventing the names of Castruccio's victims (Iacopo da Gia and Bastiano di Possente), Machiavelli describes how Castruccio took Pistoia without a struggle by receiving the leaders of the *Neri* and *Bianchi* factions amicably to lull them into a false sense of security. When the proper moment arrived, Castruccio had both men and most of their friends executed, and bereft of any serious opposition, the city bowed to his rule.[26]

Machiavelli's account of Castruccio's life substitutes his extraordinary feats of valor and deceit for the kinds of fantastic adventures that many archtypal heroes experience. Castruccio's opponents are historical ones, not mythical monsters. His reward is not the hand of a beautiful maiden but an illustrious political career crowned by the bestowal of a coveted title from the Holy Roman Empire — *Dei gratia dux Lucanorum, Lateranensis comes, sacri Romani imperii vexillifer et Pisarum vicarius generalis.*[27] His miraculous journey is not a voyage to the underworld but a political odyssey from obscurity to military fame. To the events of his birth, his youth, and his heroic adventures — all stylized to fit the pattern of the heroic life — Machiavelli adds a vivid description of his death to complete the archetypal structure, for "the last act in the biography of the hero is that of the death or departure. . . . Here the whole sense of the life is epitomized. Needless to say, the hero would be no hero if death held for him any terror; the first condition is reconciliation with the grave." [28] Castruccio's death has affinities with the fall of Cesare Borgia. In *The Prince*, Machiavelli described Borgia's failure as resulting from an extraordinary and extreme malignity of fortune. In like manner, Castruccio's death and his consequent failure to establish a lasting political empire in Tuscany and Lombardy is a result of a spiteful act of fortune. Like a fickle woman, *fortuna* gives and takes back her favors almost gratuitously. As Machiavelli had remarked in *The Prince*, "la fortuna è donna" (ch. 25). Fortune is a woman, and although man can control about half of his actions, the other half is entirely at the mercy of this goddess of chance. In the introduction to the life of Castruccio, Machiavelli advances the hypothesis that great heroes are obscurely born and exposed to beasts by their parents in order that *fortuna* may demonstrate that it is she (and not prudence) who makes men great by making her influence known at an age in the hero's life (early infancy) when it would be obvious that prudence had little or nothing to do with the man's later success. *Fortuna*, therefore, had a major role in forming the career of Castruccio, both in his infancy and in his meteoric rise to power. Now, the whimsical goddess decrees that her own crea-

tion must fall, and Castruccio is brought down by illness at
the high point of his political career:

But Fortune, hostile to his glory, when it was time to give him
life took it away from him, and interrupted those plans that for
a long time before Castruccio had intended to carry out, nor
could anything save death have prevented him from so doing. All
that day in the battle Castruccio had toiled; then when it ended,
all tired and drenched with sweat, he stopped at the gate of
Fucecchio to review his troops and to thank and receive them
personally . . . he thought it was a good general's duty to be the
first to mount his horse and the last to dismount. Thus, standing
exposed to a wind that usually rises at noon up from the Arno
(and is almost always unhealthy), he caught an icy chill; since he
paid no attention to it, as he was used to such discomforts, it was
the cause of his death.[29]

This particular battle was a product of Machiavelli's active
imagination. Castruccio actually died after the siege of Pistoia
on 3 September 1328.[30] But Machiavelli is less interested in
historical accuracy than he is in creating a literary myth. Consequently, though the historical facts are consciously reshaped,
Machiavelli's literary judgment is correct in placing the death
of Castruccio after his brilliant (though fictitious) victory, since
this sudden reversal increases the effect of the loss upon the
reader and parallels his quick rise to power ("But Castruccio
from a prisoner became like the prince of Lucca").

To dramatize the event further, Machiavelli has Castruccio deliver an eloquent speech to his heir, Pagolo Guinigi,
before his death:

If I had believed, my son, that Fortune had wanted to cut me
down in the middle of that journey's path leading to the glory
which I through my many successful deeds had promised myself
to attain, I would have toiled less and left you fewer enemies and
less envy, though a smaller state. . . . But Fortune, which wishes
to be the arbiter of all human affairs, did not grant me enough

judgment to early understand her nor enough time to be able to overcome her.[31]

J. H. Whitfield refuses to grant that Machiavelli's willful recasting of Castruccio's life has any real significance. He believes that the center of the work is the dying oration. In stressing the primary importance of the speech, Whitfield wishes to make of this entire biography an attack upon Castruccio, an argument for the middle road that Machiavelli usually rejects in political behavior, as he did in discussing Pope Julius II and Gianpaolo Baglioni in the *Discourses.*[32] Although the speech may counsel moderation and temperate actions not ordinarily recommended by Machiavelli nor exemplified by his protagonists, Whitfield's argument that Machiavelli does not admire Castruccio cannot bear close scrutiny. First of all, Whitfield uses another and later text, *The History of Florence,* to propose his antithesis of "insolent men" and the "legislator who begets *ordini* and stability." Nowhere does Machiavelli identify Castruccio with such historical villains. On the contrary, all of the examples I have analyzed argue against Machiavelli's derogatory treatment of Castruccio. Each of the many attempts to portray Castruccio as the archetypal hero would have no motivation whatsoever if Castruccio were not intended to be the "hero" of the narrative. All of Machiavelli's literary reshaping of history would have been superfluous if he had only wished to use this condottiere as a negative exemplum of how overreaching ambition must inevitably fall. More importantly from a literary point of view, the narrator never utters a word of criticism in the biography. It is Castruccio himself, in a moment of self-consciousness unusual for Machiavelli's protagonists, who recognizes his own vulnerability and who gives the "moral" of the story. Far from being one of the "insolent men" Machiavelli criticizes elsewhere, Castruccio's self-awareness is the final proof of his exemplary character. In the pattern common to the heroic life, the hero sallies forth, undergoes adventures, and returns home with some new knowledge or power.[33]

In like manner, Castruccio has grown in wisdom during the narrative and is able to extract a meaning from his own life before he dies.

Whitfield misreads Machiavelli's intentions in failing to emphasize the literary, fictitious quality of this biography. A comparison of Machiavelli's treatment of Castruccio in this work with that of *The History of Florence* (bk. 2, chs. 25–26, 29–30) makes his mythical recasting of this life history into the portrait of an archetypal prince even clearer. In this later history, Castruccio is never pictured as the superhuman figure he is in the biography. Almost every archetypal, imaginary element is corrected or eliminated to give a more truthful account. It is Uguccione (and not Castruccio) who is the victor at Montecatini (bk. 2, ch. 25). In place of the fictitious victory Machiavelli created by combining the events of two actual battles, he presents an historically accurate account of the battle of Altopascio (bk. 2, ch. 29) and a chronologically accurate narration of both the seizure of Pistoia (not by a double murder but by a siege) and of Castruccio's subsequent death. Machiavelli thus knew the true facts when he reshaped Castruccio's life to make him an exemplary hero.

The narrator continues beyond Castruccio's dying words to present his own assessment of the character. He begins with a parting *elogium*, a verbal epitaph:

Castruccio was then, according to all that we have seen, a man unusual not only in his own day but also in terms of many past times. He was physically of above average height, and every limb was perfectly proportioned to the others; and he was so gracious in bearing and so human in his dealings with others, that never did anyone who spoke with him leave dissatisfied. His hair tended toward red, and he wore it cut above his ears; and always, and at all times, even when it rained or snowed, he went bareheaded.[34]

The physical details are in complete harmony with Castruccio's moral and intellectual perfection. In the character sketches examined in previous chapters, Machiavelli usually stressed a person's moral or intellectual qualities. Here in the biography of Castruccio, physical details are similar to the stereotyped details of a medieval portrait; they are added simply because perfect physical proportions are as required of a perfect prince as a crown and a miter are of kings and of bishops. Even Castruccio's hair color and his habit of going without a hat emphasize the customary audaciousness which his actions revealed. Such physical detail is not intended to communicate historical truth; instead, it rounds off and completes the portrait of the man. As Federico Chabod stresses in a discussion of the difference between medieval historical realism (which accentuated physical details but lacked conceptual organization) and the "conceptual" realism of Renaissance historical works,

the realistic description of outward physical detail is undertaken by a Machiavelli or a Guicciardini, if at all, only inasmuch as it serves to complete the moral portrait of the man, in other words only inasmuch as it can furnish the writer with material which will help him to integrate his general assessment of the man's personality.[35]

Indeed, if one can judge from portraits of the period, Castruccio was anything but handsome.[36]

Perhaps following Plutarch's example, Machiavelli also cites a series of witty sayings which he attributes to Castruccio, since he had described his ideal condottiere as "wonderful in giving answers with a bite in them, either sharply or graciously." [37] Though these verbal examples of Castruccio's keenness of mind are cited to give the reader an insight into his personality, thirty-two of the thirty-four memorable sayings attributed by Machiavelli to Castruccio are borrowed from Diogenes Laertius's *Lives and Opinions of Eminent Philosophers*.[38] Machiavelli changes the quotations to fit his own purpose and replaces Greek with Italian names so that they do not seem out of place. Wit and skill in conversation were necessary signs of greatness in the Renaissance.[39] Although Castruccio was a medieval condottiere, Machiavelli makes him excel in this special Renaissance virtue. Like the physical details, the witty sayings of Castruccio are stylized, stereotyped expressions that could be applied to any ideal hero. They are added to the biography not because of the demands of historical verisimilitude but because their presence makes the literary portrait of Castruccio a more pleasing work of art.

In the concluding paragraph of the biography, Machiavelli gives a summary of Castruccio's achievements which is a powerful conclusion to this life story:

He lived forty-four years, and he was princely in all fortunes. . . . And because he was, when living, inferior to neither to Philip of Macedonia, Alexander's father, nor to Scipio of Rome, he died at the age of both; and without doubt he would have surpassed the one and the other if instead of Lucca he had had Macedonia or Rome for his native land.[40]

Machiavelli's fictional biography had opened with an historical correction which implicitly equated him with such great men as Moses or Romulus. He continued this conscious attempt to create a literary portrait of an archetypal hero by distorting historical fact in creating the marvelous political deeds Castruccio accomplished during his short life. He ends this extended portrait with another historical adjustment; the change in Castruccio's age at his death from forty-three to forty-four compels comparison with two great military leaders of antiquity. The connective *perché* ("because") is used as a causative conjunction here. Machiavelli thus has his hero die at the same age as Scipio Africanus or Philip of Macedonia precisely because he was inferior to neither man. No single sentence in Machiavelli's writings shows so clearly his constant desire to assimilate the great men of antiquity and their exemplary deeds to modern political practice.

Although less well known than Machiavelli's major

works, *The Life of Castruccio Castracani of Lucca* is the most impressive character sketch in all of Machiavelli's writings. It is a work nourished by historical fact, although it does not intend to be an historically accurate narrative. From the raw material of history and legend, Machiavelli has created a mythical protagonist intended to embody the universally recognized elements of an heroic life. Contrary to Whitfield's thesis, Machiavelli did not make "mistakes" in this biography; he consciously reshaped historical facts, as he announced in the beginning lines of the work, to present the portrait of the archetypal leader. Furthermore, this is precisely what his audience expected, since such creative distortion of historical fact for pleasing and instructional effects was viewed as the proper task of the historian or biographer. Zanobi Buondelmonti, one of the men to whom Machiavelli dedicated the work, wrote to him and commented on the manuscript. Even though Buondelmonti immediately recognized many of the sayings Machiavelli attributed to Castruccio as borrowings from classical literature, he felt that the work was an excellent piece of historical writing. He criticized Machiavelli not for falsifying history with these quotations but for not doing a better job of it, since he believed that many of the quotations lacked "that vivacity . . . that greatness that one would require of so great a man." [41] Since Castruccio was supposed to be an outstanding man, Machiavelli's contemporaries expected him to fashion everything about the biography in such a way that it reflected his greatness. Such an audience was not composed of professional historians who would question Machiavelli's historical accuracy. They were learned men who read history or biography for pleasure and moral instruction. As Scholes and Kellogg have noted, history and biography directed toward such an audience "tend to move away from merely chronological narrative toward more esthetically satisfying patterns. This means, in effect, that historical narrative will borrow mythical or fictional means of articulation to the extent that it is willing to sacrifice science to art" (p. 217). In borrowing the archetypal structure of the heroic life from legend and literature, Machiavelli was able to make his biography of Castruccio Castracani a work of art, a work which surely presented an esthetically satisfying picture of the perfect hero within the Machiavellian framework of political ideas.

After writing *The Prince* and the *Discourses*, Machiavelli turned more to historical and literary topics. The importance of these two theoretical treatises has led critics to see the later works as somehow less important, as secondary literary efforts of a mind better suited to political theory. Even such a sensitive critic as Federico Chabod believes that Machiavelli's later writings on history reflect a "new sense of disillusionment and self-withdrawal. . . . Little by little, slowly but without pause, Machiavelli's imagination slides back into the past, loses its creative vigour and assumes the form of an interpretative faculty." [42] I believe that all Machiavelli's writings (and especially his later historical works) can and must be treated as literature, and that in the limited area of Machiavelli's art of portraiture, these works are the culmination of a long series of developments beginning during his diplomatic career. In the portrait of Castruccio, Machiavelli presents the picture of a man whose life embodied the elements of the heroic life pattern. It is in no sense simply a preliminary exercise for *The History of Florence*, but several important stylistic features of this biography will reappear in the most powerful portraits of that history. With Castruccio, Machiavelli's art of portraiture comes of age, and this maturity will be evident in some of the more complex character sketches he uses in recounting the history of his native city.

VI

The History of Florence: *Character Sketches in Humanist History*

In *The History of Florence*, Machiavelli combines the art of portraiture he had already practiced in other works with the framework of humanist historiography. The whole spectrum of his previous analyses of historical figures can be found in the work, from simple remarks on a man's traits reminiscent of the search for the "nature of the man" in the dispatches to more stylized, and more successful, portraits of important individuals presented in greater detail. As we have already noted, Machiavelli places his own history of Florence within the humanist tradition, continuing the work of Leonardo Bruni and Poggio Bracciolini, who were also members of the Florentine Chancellery.[1] Machiavelli believed that these most excellent historians lacked a proper understanding of Florentine internal affairs, but he agrees with them (and their classical models) that history is a literary genre which should both please and instruct. Such a definition of history (or indeed of literature) was common in the Renaissance, but few men took the idea so seriously as Machiavelli. The lives and deeds of great men play a didactic role in all of his non-fictional works. Machiavelli seems to have concluded that more studied treatment of important individuals than was normally possible in the theoretical works would have a greater impact upon the reader. His biography of Castruccio Castracani was his first attempt to portray a character in depth and was a great artistic success. The commission from Cardinal Giulio de'

Medici (later Pope Clement VII) to write a history of Florence gave Machiavelli the opportunity to treat at length many important figures in the history of his beloved city-state. He states in the preface to the history that more description is advisable if the writer wishes to delight as well as teach: "If anything pleases or teaches in history, it is that which is described in detail." [2] Though some critics have found what they consider to be structural or conceptual flaws in this work, none of their arguments seriously affect the artistic merits of Machiavelli's work.[3] The fact that Machiavelli continues the mature style of portraiture that he employed so brilliantly in *The Life of Castruccio Castracani* in this historical study explains in part its appeal to the contemporary reader and its status as a classic of Renaissance historiography.

Felix Gilbert asserts that Machiavelli used humanist patterns of historiography in *The History of Florence* only as a framework for his own political message.[4] Although the book contains such typical humanist components as invented speeches and a discourse on the origin of the city, Machiavelli's history is not a simple exercise in humanist historiography. As one might expect from a reading of his other works, the truly fascinating episodes in his history involve the examinations of important historical protagonists. Within the framework of history, Machiavelli succeeds in creating literary portraits which alone would justify a reading of this work. Although he treats many of the same events described in the works of Villani and Compagni, two medieval chroniclers of Florentine history, he avoids the often chaotic organization of those works and their lack of selectivity.[5] While Villani and Compagni narrate almost any detail of their city's history, no matter how insignificant, Machiavelli selects his material to exclude all but major internal and foreign political affairs. The working of a divine Providence within human history that these two medieval historians saw in Florence is also conspicuously absent in *The History of Florence*. In such a work, historical figures have an implicitly didactic purpose. Avoiding a direct statement of opinion, the narrator often uses historical personalities to underline theoretical ideas which he feels history can teach the reader. One of the main themes in the work is the decadence of modern times, this "wasted world" as Machiavelli calls it. There is an increasingly elegiac tone in the work as Machiavelli moves from the great period of Florentine history and the deeds of outstanding men closer to his own day when foreign influences had already begun to erode Florentine hegemony in central Italy. In spite of this increasingly pessimistic note which sets his history apart from the essentially optimistic earlier works, Machiavelli did, however, believe that Florentine history could at least offer a series of negative exempla to avoid:

And if, in describing the events that occurred in this wasted world, the bravery of the soldier, the courage of the captain, or the patriotism of the citizen are not recorded, one shall be able to see with what artifices, deceits, and cunning princes, soldiers, and leaders of republics conducted themselves in order to maintain a reputation that they did not deserve. This, perhaps, will not be less useful than an acquaintance of ancient history, for if the latter incites the noble mind to imitation, the former will demonstrate what to avoid or to stifle [bk. 5, ch. 1].[6]

Historical protagonists are thus implicit exempla in this work, but they are presented in a manner different from the explicit models in *The Prince* and the *Discourses*. The distinction between character sketches as symbolic figures in those works and character sketches in this history is primarily stylistic. Sketches used as explicit exempla are those described by the narrator as models to be imitated or avoided. Consequently, their style is set more clearly within a didactic framework; the narrator addresses the reader directly, instructing him to note points in the portrait which he feels are worthy of special attention. This direct dialog between reader and narrator was very evident in, for example, Machiavelli's treatment of Borgia in *The Prince*. Machiavelli's historical portraits are no less didactic in purpose, but the narrator's judgments and opinions are less obvious, though ever present in the selection of the "facts" he chooses to present. Though many of the historical figures in this work may exemplify some of Machiavelli's favorite political maxims, they are never "types without individual reality" as Gilbert states.[7] Gilbert also believes that Machiavelli's approach to history is a direct outgrowth of medieval allegorical commentary.[8] But, in a manner similar to his method in the theoretical treatises, Machiavelli's historical subjects function in two ways. They are both actual historical characters whose deeds are part of the city's history and illustrations of certain universal personalities or situations through their actions. The allegorical method, which subordinates the literal meaning to the figurative meaning (often intentionally obscure), is simply not present in Machiavelli's works. The literal sense of the narrative is never a fiction devised to conceal a second or primary meaning. Both levels of meaning are true; each is simply considered on a different level of analysis.[9] With the exception of some transparent minor distortions such as the quotation of falsified casualty figures to criticize the use of mercenary troops[10] or simple factual errors, Machiavelli does intend *The History of Florence* to be a reasonably accurate history of his city. But historical accuracy does not eliminate his own particular style of presenting major historical figures.

Often in the work Machiavelli describes memorable episodes which he felt were noteworthy not because of their intrinsic historical importance but because they illustrated admirable character traits in action. He had already learned to use such vignettes to great effect in the *Discourses,* as in his account of the bravery of the Countess Caterina at Forlì (bk. 3, ch. 6). Consider, for instance, his brief picture of Biagio del Melano in *The History of Florence.* Biagio was charged with the defense of the Florentine fortress of Monte Petroso. Beseiged by Milanese forces, and seeing no method of saving the fort for Florence, Biagio threw cloth and straw against the side of the citadel which was not yet burning and tossed his children down to safety, saying to the enemy: "Take for yourselves those goods which Fortune has bestowed upon me and of which it is possible for you to deprive me; those which I have from my courage, in which my honor and glory consist, I shall not give up nor can you take away" (bk. 4, ch. 12).[11] The Milanese, amazed by such *virtù*, ran to save his children and pleaded with Biagio to save himself. He refused, preferring to die rather than to live owing his life to his city's enemies. Machiavelli is overwhelmed by admiration for such courage and loyalty, terming Biagio's actions an "exemplum truly worthy of that praised antiquity, and so much more admirable than ancient deeds since it is so unusual today" (bk. 4, ch. 12).[12] To highlight Biagio's deed, Machiavelli pairs this event with another, the account of the treachery of another Florentine, Zanobi del Pino, under similar circumstances. While both Biagio's enemies and the city of Florence honored his courage and loyalty by protecting and raising his children, Zanobi's cowardice was so vile that his enemies killed him in disgust after he had surrendered to them:

Agnolo della Pergola, not being able to suffer the cowardice and the evil nature of Zanobi, gave him as a booty of war to his servants, who, after many insults, gave him nothing to eat but paper printed with snakes, saying that they wanted to change him from Guelf to Ghibelline; and fasting in such a manner, he died in a few days [bk. 4, ch. 12].[13]

Biagio's courage made him equal the great deeds of famous ancient heroes; Zanobi's cowardice was so vile that his enemies killed him by making him eat paper imprinted with the Visconti coat of arms (the *biscie* or snakes). The choice of this "food" ironically underlines Zanobi's deceitfulness, for the serpent has symbolized treachery since the biblical story of Adam and Eve. The imaginary speeches Machiavelli often inserts into his narrative were an accepted part of classical or humanist histories, but Machiavelli never allows his discourses to become simple rhetorical exercises. In Biagio's brief words, and in his death, we find the typically Machiavellian approach to politics, the refusal of easy compromise or a middle course which lesser men would have chosen. Alessandro Montevecchi notes that many of Machiavelli's imaginary speeches emphasize this dramatic tension between a given situation and two diametrically opposed responses to it.[14] Biagio's brief speech sets up absolute alternatives: worldly goods and Fortune are opposed to courage, glory, and honor. Biagio then makes the only choice open to a Machiavellian hero, an absolute choice which avoids a middle path.

Another vignette portrays the dramatic rise to power of Michele di Lando, a wool-comber who assumed control of the Florentine government for a brief time after the Ciompi revolt of 1378. As a mob formed outside the city hall, Michele mounted the steps, barefoot and with scarcely any clothes on his back, and told the crowd: "You see: this palace is now yours, and this city is in your hands. What do you think you ought to do now?" (bk. 3, ch. 16).[15] Struck by the man's nobility (though he was a commoner by birth and by dress), the crowd gave him the reins of government. Machiavelli's imagination is clearly aroused by this dramatic act; he felt that Michele gained the favor of the crowd solely because he was "a wise and prudent man, more favored by nature than by fortune" (bk. 3, ch. 16).[16] His innate talents are thus clearly contrasted to his outer appearance. He is shoeless and almost in rags, but his *virtù* is apparent even to the mob. Such a scene is reminiscent of the legendary Cincinnatus, the proverbial symbol of republican patriotism, who left his rude plow to lead Rome in defense of its liberty. Machiavelli intended that the example of Michele be viewed in a similar manner. Because Michele di Lando was superior to any other Florentine citizen in courage, goodness, and prudence, Machiavelli wanted to preserve his memory for the edification of posterity in spite of his plebian origins: "And he merits being listed among the few who have benefited their fatherland" (bk. 3, ch. 17).[17]

Such brief vignettes are common in the work, but the most characteristic method of examining a figure is an *elogium* which is added to the narration of the man's actions.[18] Although an *elogium* is not necessarily written in praise of a man after his death, Machiavelli usually bestows such praise or blame as a kind of epitaph, rendered after the individual has passed from the historical scene. He first uses this technique in his biography of Castruccio Castracani, extending the *elogium* at great length to embellish his mythical portrait of the archetypal hero. Such a summary statement may simply be attached to a description of the man's deeds with little attention to how the man's life and his *elogium* are connected. In the best character sketches, however, the *elogium* is integrally linked to the preceding narrative and may contain, besides an evaluation of the character's deeds, an examination of his moral qualities, memorable sayings attributed to him, parting words of advice to his loved ones, and even symbolic physical details. Several aspects of the descriptive style used in the biography of Castruccio thus reappear in portraits of *The History of Florence*.

Examples of the brief, uncomplicated *elogium* are frequent, usually found in parts of the narrative where Machiavelli attempts to span events of many years in only a few chapters and combines both internal events and foreign affairs. These discursive (rather than analytic) portions of the book seem to have been regarded by Machiavelli as filler, as factual information he felt he had to include in the history but which interested him less than periods dominated by striking individuals who deserved more lengthy treatment. Consequently, when a man who has done something of note appears in the history, Machiavelli pauses to comment on his deeds before returning to his chronological narrative. Such is his method in referring to Corso Donati and Giovanni de' Medici. Each was important in the history of Florence, though hardly as significant as the figures Machiavelli treats at greater length. Machiavelli views Corso, the chief of the *Neri* faction, as the type of partisan leader who kept Florence in constant turmoil throughout her history. Machiavelli isolates a single dominant trait in Corso and then shows how that attribute explained his life and death. Corso's nature was quarrelsome, his major quality a restless spirit (*animo inquieto:* bk. 2, ch. 22). In this respect, he is not unlike Appius Claudius in the *Discourses.* Because of his restless nature, Corso used any excuse to instigate mischief and was always at odds with whoever ruled the city:

In order to give himself a reputation, he always had an opinion contrary to that held by the most powerful; and wherever he saw the people lean toward, there he turned to make himself more popular; so that he was the leader of all disputes and new schemes, and to him flocked all those who wished to obtain anything extraordinary [bk. 2, ch. 22].[19]

His end was as violent as his life, for he was set upon by his rivals and his throat was cut in the ensuing scuffle. To this brief glance at a man whose factionalism was symbolic of Florence's constant problems, Machiavelli adds a sad summary *elogium:* "Such was the end of Corso . . . and if he had possessed a cooler spirit, his memory would be happier; nevertheless he merits to be numbered among the most distinguished citizens that our city ever had" (bk. 2, ch. 23).[20] Machiavelli's regret for the waste of this man's talents in petty squabbles is evident in the elegiac tone of his closing remarks. This brief sketch serves only to immortalize the memory of a man whose deeds were representative of typical aspects of Florentine history. The *elogium* in this instance is a verbal epitaph presented to save Corso's memory from the erosion of time. Such a purpose must have been one of the reasons why history or biography was ever written. Such an *elogium* enables Machiavelli to evaluate the merits of an individual, but there is little art in its presentation.

Of greater interest is the more elaborate *elogium.* An entire chapter (bk. 4, ch. 16) is devoted to an evaluation of Giovanni de' Medici. Its theme is Giovanni's moderation and how such a quality led to his family's political successes, setting the pattern that his son Cosimo followed. When Cosimo's descendents openly asserted their authority, something Giovanni or Cosimo never did, they began to meet serious opposition. Machiavelli's imaginary speeches rarely represent a simple imitation of classical or humanist historical rhetoric; they are more often a means of strengthening his own theoretical arguments or of embellishing his character sketches. In his portrait of Giovanni, Machiavelli first fashions a speech which he has Giovanni deliver from his deathbed to his sons. This dying oration is carefully designed so that political temperance is the dying man's parting advice:

Concerning matters of state, if you wish to live in security, take only such a portion of power as the laws and your citizens would give you: thus you will avoid both envy and danger, for it is not what is given to a man, but what he has taken, which causes hatred; . . . By using these devices I have, in the midst of so many enemies and conflicting opinions, not only maintained but increased my reputation in this city. In following my footsteps, you will maintain and increase your own reputations [bk. 4, ch. 16].[21]

Machiavelli's concluding evaluation of Giovanni is far more studied than the *elogium* of either Corso Donati or Michele di Lando:

Giovanni was compassionate, and not only did he give alms to those who asked for them, but often he relieved the burdens of the poor without being asked. He loved all, he praised the good and had compassion on the evil. He never sought honors and yet he had them all. He never went to the palace unless he was summoned. He loved peace and avoided war. He provided relief to men in adversity and aided them in prosperity. He was never a despoiler of public wealth but was always instrumental in increasing the commonwealth. In public affairs, he was courteous; not of great eloquence but a man of the greatest prudence. He was melancholy in appearance, but after a time in conversation he grew pleasing and facetious. He died a very rich man, but richer still in good fame and the best wishes of mankind. His estate, both the wealth and the respect he left behind him, was not only maintained but was increased by his son Cosimo [bk. 4, ch. 16].[22]

In the original Italian, this carefully patterned paragraph is constructed around the rhetorical figures of antithesis ("Non domandò mai onori ed ebbegli tutti. . . . Amava la pace, fuggiva la guerra") and chiasmus ("Era alieno dalle rapine publiche e del bene commune aumentatore").[23] Such devices, referring to the polar extremes in political conduct Giovanni avoided, help to render (rather than simply state) Giovanni's moderate behavior, drawing attention to the drastic courses of action he rejected. This careful attention to the structure of the *elogium* sets it apart from the shorter vignettes we have previously examined. The portrait is also evidence of Machiavelli's political realism. Though his temperament compelled him to prefer drastic, absolute political decisions to weak compromises, if moderation becomes the key to the retention of political power (as he feels it was for Giovanni or Cosimo de' Medici), it is praised.

Giovanni's portrait is stylistically similar to Machiavelli's greatest character sketches in *The History of Florence* and is a step beyond the brief passages devoted to Biagio del Melano, Corso Donati, and Michele di Lando. Since this history was commissioned by a Medici prelate, it is not surprising that two of the three most arresting sketches in the work are those of Cosimo de' Medici and his son Lorenzo Il Magnifico. Though he has often been accused of servile flattery, Machiavelli does not ignore the faults of these men. Both were, after all, the main characters in the most brilliant epoch of Florentine history. Modern historians uninfluenced by Medici patronage devote equal or even greater amounts of space to their accomplishments. Aware of the possible charge of flattery, Machiavelli anticipated it in his dedication to Pope Clement VII, explicitly denying any such intention.[24] Cosimo's entrance into Machiavelli's history is forecast long before the death of his father Giovanni:

It is certainly true that whenever through fortune of the city a wise, good, and powerful citizen appears (which seldom occurs) who establishes laws by means of which the dissension of the nobility and the people may be restrained or prevented from causing harm, then the government of the city may be called stable and secure [bk. 4, ch. 1].[25]

Machiavelli uses Cosimo to illustrate such a "wise, good, and powerful citizen." Following his father's advice, Cosimo retained control of Florence from behind the scenes, never allowing his power to become too obvious. Though his authority was pervasive, he never held an important elective political office. In books 4 through 6, Machiavelli's account of the external and internal affairs of the Florentine republic presents ample evidence that Cosimo was the prototype of the perfect civil ruler, the just lawgiver whose ability to quiet factional strife while retaining at least the façade of democratic government is contrasted to the despotism of tyrants, the *uomini insolenti* like Walter, the Duke of Athens, with whom he is compared.[26] Again, as he had done with Giovanni, Machiavelli employs a carefully patterned *elogium* to summarize Cosimo's character and achievements, an *elogium* which complements the preceding historical details:

Cosimo was the most renowned and illustrious citizen outside of the military profession that ever lived, not only in Florence but also in any other city of which we have a record: because he not only surpassed all those of his times in wealth and authority but also in generosity and prudence; and among those qualities which contributed to make him prince of his native land, the most important were his generosity and his magnificence [bk. 7, ch. 1].[27]

Cosimo's liberality was revealed completely only after his death, when it was discovered that there was hardly a man in Florence who had not received gifts from him or loans which had never been repaid. His magnificence was a matter of public record and was evident everywhere in the splendid public works he donated to the city. Faithful to his father's directions, he always governed indirectly and moderately:

And although his private homes, and all his other works and actions, were of a princely nature, and he alone in Florence was prince, nevertheless everything was tempered by his prudence so that he never transgressed civil modesty: in his conversation, his servants, his traveling, his mode of life, and in his relations, he was always similar to the average citizen; for he knew that a constant display of pomp causes more envy among men than those actions tempered with honesty and lack of ostentation [bk. 7, ch. 5].[28]

As he had done in his summary description of Castruccio Castracani, Machiavelli embellishes his portrait of Cosimo by a reference to his physical appearance and to his manner in his personal dealings. Here, as in that biography, the physical details correspond to his other qualities:

He was of middle stature with an olive complexion and a venerable aspect. He was not learned but was exceedingly eloquent and gifted with a natural prudence, and was therefore generous to his friends, compassionate to the poor, sharp in conversation, cautious in advice, quick in his executions, and witty and serious in his sayings and replies [bk. 7, ch. 6].[29]

His medium height, lack of pedantic erudition, and his courteous, open relations with others match perfectly his character as an unobtrusive power behind the scenes in Florence. Unlike Castruccio's manner, which was spectacular and which required a vivid symbolic physical description for its complement, Cosimo's character is symbolized by unassuming physical details. Again as in the portrait of Castruccio, Machiavelli underlines Cosimo's skill in conversation and his wit by citing some of his humorous remarks. When his wife asked him shortly before his death why he kept his eyes closed, he replied that he was only practicing in order to get used to the idea (bk. 7, ch. 6). When some Florentines complained to him after his return from exile that he was ruining the city by banishing so many good citizens who were his political enemies (an action they took to be an act against God), he answered that "it was better to have a damaged city than to lose it; that two yards of rose-colored cloth were sufficient to make a gentleman; and that states were not held with rosary beads in hand" (bk. 7, ch. 6).[30] Such clever remarks do more than reveal Cosimo's skill in conversation. They also show that Machiavelli considered Cosimo to be a political realist, a man whose political philosophy was similar to his own in caring more for the real foundations of political power than for its symbolic trappings. Aware that his subject was a prince in all but name, Machiavelli justified his elevated style in the portrait of Cosimo by the importance of the man:

If, in writing about the deeds of Cosimo, I have imitated those who write about the lives of princes rather than those who write about general history, it need not cause any amazement, for having been such an extraordinary man in our city's history, I was compelled to praise him by extraordinary means [bk. 7, ch. 6].[31]

As in the sketch of Castruccio, Machiavelli makes the summary evaluation and *elogium* an integral part of his historical narrative. The character's actions foreshadow his moral, intellectual, and physical traits, all of which in turn reflect the implicit evaluation of the man contained in the motivated facts Machiavelli selects to portray his life and deeds.

Lorenzo de' Medici is treated in the last chapter of *The History of Florence*. In contrast to his presentation of Cosimo, Machiavelli's view of Lorenzo's actions is far more critical. His overreaching, ambitious nature is revealed indirectly by a remark he attributes to Lorenzo's brother, Giuliano, to make his judgment of Lorenzo seem more credible: "Giuliano often complained of this to his brother, Lorenzo, saying that he was afraid that by wanting too much, they would lose all" (bk. 8, ch. 2).[32] It was the wiser Giuliano, and not Lorenzo, who was later to pay the price of his brother's ambitious nature in the Pazzi conspiracy. It was Machiavelli's opinion that Lorenzo's impetuous nature and his overbearing attitude (completely contrary to the example of Giovanni or Cosimo) caused the conspiracy: "Nevertheless Lorenzo, full of youth and power, wanted to direct everything and wanted everything to show his influence. The Pazzi family, with all their nobility and their wealth, were not able to bear so many affronts, and they began to think about some way of revenging themselves" (bk. 8, ch. 3).[33] Machiavelli also notes that the siege of Volterra and the resulting pillage of that rebel city in 1472, an action that permanently alienated the town when moderation would have retained its loyalty, was solely Lorenzo's responsibility (bk. 8, ch. 30). He is even so bold as to imply that the Pazzi conspiracy failed because the Medici money had made Florence "deaf" to liberty (bk. 8, ch. 8), this in a work commissioned by a Medici pope. In spite of these defects, Lorenzo's greatness was undeniable. Machiavelli mentions Lorenzo's generosity, his public works, his festivals and patronage of the arts and letters, his extreme fortune in political affairs, his wit and eloquence, and his speediness in following his intentions with action. Machiavelli is puzzled, however, by the mixture of such exemplary moral and intellectual qualities with Lorenzo's remarkable penchant for pleasures of the flesh (cose veneree) or for what he considered childish pastimes (giuochi puerili). Machiavelli felt that there was such a contrast of personality traits in Lorenzo's character that "one saw in him two different persons, joined in an almost impossible union" (bk. 8, ch. 36).[34] Conspicuously absent from this sketch is any of the symbolic physical description we have found in other portraits. Perhaps Machiavelli was wise in omitting such a reference here, for Lorenzo was not a handsome man. Any physical description that matched Lorenzo's marvelous abilities would have appeared a transparent falsification to a reader. Indeed, in a humorous letter relating his encounter with an ugly prostitute, Machiavelli had earlier compared her mouth with Lorenzo's.[35] Though the *elogium* of Lorenzo covers the same topics as those devoted to Giovanni or Cosimo, its presentation is less carefully constructed and lacks the tight organization that concentrated the summary evaluations of Giovanni or Cosimo into a unified, compact paragraph.

The sketches of these three Medici "heroes" are important examples of Machiavelli's mature art of portraiture, but the most successful portrait in the work is that of a "villain," one of the *uomini insolenti* who are the polar opposites of Cosimo de' Medici. Machiavelli uses the story of Walter, the Duke of Athens, in *The History of Florence* (bk. 2, chs. 33–37) as a concrete proof of the theory, mentioned many times in other works, that men change rulers gladly, hoping for improvement through novelty. In an earlier chapter, Machiavelli had noted how the duke had ruled Florence briefly in 1326 for Duke Charles of Calabria, when the city's people had accepted his protection to defend themselves against Castruccio Castracani. There he hinted that the duke's moderate behavior during that short period was contrary to his true nature: "His conduct was nevertheless modest and contrary to his nature, so that everyone loved him" (bk. 2, ch. 30).[36] The duke's second entrance into the narrative is colored by a preface suggesting impending doom: "The duke arrived in Florence just at that moment when the undertaking against Lucca had completely failed, as if the gods had wanted to prepare things for future evils" (bk. 2, ch. 33).[37] Because of his desire to make this sketch dramatic as well as historical, Machiavelli only gradually uncovers the personal characteristics of this tyrant. First, the desire of the Florentine nobility to use the duke as their tool against their political opponents causes the duke's innate but latent lust for personal, despotic power to come to

the surface as he realizes his opportunity to exploit the selfish-
ness of the nobles for his own purposes. The narrator gives the
reader a privileged view into the duke's mind in the description
of his reaction to their offer of support: "These arguments ex-
cited the ambitious mind of the duke to a greater desire of
power" (bk. 2, ch. 33).[38] To illustrate the duke's powers of
dissimulation, Machiavelli reveals to the reader the hidden
motives for his prosecution of the leaders of the ill-fated Luccan
campaign: "In order to gain for himself the reputation of being
severe and just, by this means increasing his favor with the
plebians, he prosecuted those who had conducted the war
against Lucca; and he put to death Giovanni de' Medici, Naddo
Rucellai, and Guglielmo Altoviti, and condemned many to
pay fines and to go into exile" (bk. 2, ch. 33).[39] The duke's
nature is also laid bare as the narrator explains why he chose
to lodge in a convent: "The duke had, in order to give himself
a greater appearance of religion and humanity, chosen the
convent of the Minor Friars of Santa Croce for his residence"
(bk. 2, ch. 34).[40] Although he praised the same qualities of
deceitfulness and cunning in the characters of Cesare Borgia or
Castruccio Castracani, Machiavelli opposes the Duke of Athens's cleverness because it is motivated solely by petty self-
interest.

In the speech of the Signoria to the duke, which
Machiavelli uses to foreshadow the tyrant's downfall, the advice
of the anonymous speaker renders one of Machiavelli's favorite
maxims, here expressed by an historical figure in an historical
context:

And this we advise you, reminding you that only that dominion
which is voluntary is durable; nor should you wish, blinded by a
little ambition, to place yourself in an untenable position from
which you cannot extricate yourself and where you must of necessity
fall with great injury to both you and us [bk. 2, ch. 34].[41]

In spite of the timely warning of this speech, the duke's arrogant, power-hungry nature will not allow him to moderate his desire for total power: "These words did not in the least soften the hardened spirit of the duke" (bk. 2, ch. 35).[42] Having depicted an individual characterized by lust for power, Machiavelli shows the resulting developments to be logical consequences of this attribute: the duke sets up a tyranny which finally drives the people to rebellion. The moral of this entire episode — Machiavelli's belief that only authority voluntarily given is durable — is contained in the anonymous speech, but the advice of the speaker, presented in the form of an historical speech, does not have the same blunt, didactic effect that a narrator's opinion would have produced if it had been injected into the story. Although we are always aware of his presence, the narrator is never overinsistent in his judgments. His opinions are always fashioned to appear to be self-evident conclusions from the "facts" he has chosen to report.

After the Duke of Athens is driven from the city, Machiavelli evaluates his actions and personality. The closing passages of this sketch show again a continuation of several techniques also used in the description of Castruccio Castracani. First, Machiavelli presents a final verdict on the man which is added to the enumeration of his evil deeds: "This duke, as his actions demonstrated, was avaricious and cruel; difficult to deal with in audiences, haughty in his responses; he desired the slavery of men and not their good will; and because of this he desired more to be feared than to be loved" (bk. 2, ch. 37).[43] To this, he attaches a short description of the Duke of Athens's physical appearance which complements his baseness, just as the description of Castruccio's perfect physical proportions corresponded to his moral perfection:

Nor was his appearance any less despicable than his manners, because he was small, black, and he had a long, thin beard: so that he deserved to be hated in every respect, and at the end of ten months his evil deeds lost him the power that the evil advice of others had given him [bk. 2, ch. 37].[44]

The man is "small" and "black" in both a literal and a figurative sense. Such symbolic physical description, hardly intended as an accurate account of the man's appearance, is the perfect ending for the sketch of the perfect villain. A blending of several devices — insights into the Duke of Athens's mind showing his ambition and tyrannical nature, descriptions of his deeds that illustrate his nature dynamically, and the symbolic use of physical details — are all used to sketch a portrait which not only communicates an historical lesson but also represents a truly literary creation.

VII *Machiavelli's Fictional Characters*

The portraiture in Machiavelli's nonfictional or historical works is only one aspect of a major preoccupation in all of his writings. The same literary impulse that inspired Machiavelli to fill his theoretical works with sketches of fascinating historical individuals also created a number of memorable literary figures in his two major comedies — *Mandragola* (1518) and *Clizia* (1524–1525) — as well as in *Belfagor* (1515–1520), his single novella.[1] The similarities between Machiavelli's portraiture and his analysis of character in his political or historical works and in his literary works is striking, but it should not be surprising. Machiavelli thought of himself as both a poet and a political theorist. In a letter to Lodovico Alamanni (17 December 1517), he laments the fact that Ariosto had not placed him among the many poets listed in his *Orlando furioso*:

> Today I read Ariosto's *Orlando furioso*, and the poem is truly all beautiful, and in many places it is marvelous. If he is there, give him my regards, and tell him that I am only sorry that, having remembered so many poets, he left me out like a nobody; for I shall not treat him in my *Golden Ass* as he treated me in his *Orlando*.[2]

Posterity has forgiven Ariosto for his oversight and has agreed with his implicit judgment that most of Machiavelli's poems were written by a man who had little talent for lyrical expression, but this judgment should not obscure Machiavelli's talents in other literary pursuits. As Machiavelli's most recent biographer puts it, few Italians (or few writers from any nation) have excelled in more than one literary genre, but Machiavelli was successful in almost all he explored:

An incomparable political and historical writer, he wrote only one novella, but that of outstanding merit. He wrote only one play arising spontaneously from his own inspiration, not from the importunity of friends or worked up for an occasion on the basis of Latin models; and with it he produced the best comedy in the whole of the Italian theatre . . . the best play any modern author had written up to then, and perhaps the best Italian play of all time.[3]

When these literary masterpieces are combined with Machiavelli's private letters — a body of correspondence which reflects a "tone of immediacy, of relaxed intimacy," in the words of one critic, that was "without precedent and indeed has had few rivals then or since" [4] — the result is a remarkable collection of works which justifies Machiavelli's own high estimation of his artistic talents.

  Belfagor provides an instructive example of how Machiavelli analyzes his fictional characters. Machiavelli enjoyed some reputation as a storyteller, and it is regrettable that *Belfagor* is the only story he completed.[5] It is equally unfortunate that his literary works are too often "picked over for material that will help in the erection of some monument to his fame as a political, military, or historical writer . . . all too seldom have they been judged as works of art." [6] Gilberto Paolini, for example, believes that the humor in the story is only superficial and that its purpose is a serious one, presenting elements of Machiavelli's misogamy, misogyny, and his belief in the gullibility of the *volgo*.[7] Luigi Russo's reading of the work touches upon literary problems, but Paolini's argument that the story is essentially concerned with the credulity of men is taken from Russo.[8] Bàrberi Squarotti, in his tenacious attempts to find a "tragic" structure in all of Machiavelli's writings, reads the work as a tragedy.[9] It is unlikely that Machiavelli intended the novella to be read with his theoretical works as a key to its meaning. In spite of the fact that the story may contain several of Machiavelli's favorite ideas, *Belfagor* is primarily an extremely funny story, intended to amuse the reader by recounting the predicament of a devil who was sent to earth to take a wife to investigate the complaints of the damned that their wives were responsible for their damnation.

Machiavelli portrays the protagonist of the novella through the words of other characters rather than by giving the reader a direct judgment of the narrator. The tale opens with an infernal council scene, a gathering of the princes of hell. The central event of this infernal council is a speech by Pluto. Completely unlike Dante's *Inferno* where the atmosphere still inspires awe in the believer, and totally lacking the majesty of Milton's hell, Machiavelli's infernal council is a gathering of Renaissance courtiers whose relationships are governed by courtesy and decorum:[10]

My very dear friends, since by heavenly decree and unchangeable destiny I possess this kingdom, and because of this I cannot be obliged to submit to any earthly or heavenly judgment, nevertheless, because the best proof of prudence in those who hold great power is to submit themselves to the rule of law and to value the opinions of others, I have decided to ask your advice on how I should act in a matter that could cause shame to our rule. For since all the souls of men who come into our kingdom say that their wives were the cause, and as this seems impossible to us, I am afraid that if we accept their explanation we could be slandered as being too credulous, and if we do not, as being lenient and poor friends of justice. And since one is the vice of the frivolous while the other is that of the unjust, and since we wish to avoid being blamed for either, but not being able to find the means, we have called you together so that you may aid us with your advice in order that this realm, which has always lived free from scandal in the past, may continue to do so in the future.[11]

The presentation of Pluto's character (implicitly that of all devils, including Belfagor) through his own words in this opening speech anticipates the story's structure — a double transformation of the diabolic into the human and the human into the diabolic. The opening sentence is a perfect unconscious revelation of the devils' pride and arrogance, the reason for which God originally cast them into hell. Pluto's assertion that he cannot be subject to any heavenly judgment is as hollow as the bombastic speeches of Milton's devils. The long, drawn-out first sentence suggests Pluto's pomposity and blindness to his own limitations, which all the devils share. The closing phrase, referring to Pluto's belief that his kingdom has always been well regarded, only adds to the ridiculousness of his words. The ruler of hell's legendary pride in his power is thus satirized in his own speech. He reveals himself to be as anxious over public opinion as are ordinary men.

The initial monolog gives the reader the key to the character of Pluto and his follower Belfagor. The speech makes the region of hell and its inhabitants appear in a comic light and implies that Belfagor may be a target for the very astute humans, Onesta and Gianmatteo, whom he will encounter on earth. The devils are humanized, a transformation underlined by the use of the word *uomini* to refer to hell's inhabitants. The naïveté of Pluto's speech hints that except for the devils' God-given positions of authority in hell, both the damned and their captors suffer from the same basic vices and limitations. Machiavelli's technique is one of "defamiliarization" or of "making strange." [12] Here, of course, the strangeness lies not in hell's infernal character but in precisely the human, ordinary, mundane aspects with which it is endowed by the narrator.

After the opening speech, the reader is prepared for the catastrophes that ensue when Belfagor assumes human form as Roderigo and marries Onesta, an ironic name indeed in view of her subsequent actions. After the marriage, the devil finds that being a husband is even worse than being an underling in hell: "Madonna Onesta had brought to Roderigo's house not only her noble background and her beauty but also as much pride as Lucifer ever had: and Roderigo, who had experienced both, judged his wife's pride to be greater." [13] Besides the crushing debts Onesta incurred, her insolent nature drove all of Roderigo's servants out of his house after only a few days. Forced to live in such a "hellish" situation, even his family (actually, other devils he had brought from hell to give the appearance of a normal household) preferred eternal damnation to life near Onesta: "These devils, whom Roderigo had brought with him as his family, preferred to return to hell and to be in its fire rather than to live in the world under her rule." [14]

While the devils become humanized, the human characters assume diabolic proportions. After running away from Onesta and the ruinous debts incurred on her behalf, Belfagor meets another figure, Gianmatteo del Brica, who rescues him from his creditors in return for a promise of great riches. Their plan is simple: Belfagor will enter a woman's body and will cause her to appear possessed; Gianmatteo will then pose as an exorciser of spirits and will receive a reward for freeing the woman of her malady. This charade occurs several times, making Gianmatteo a wealthy man, but Belfagor vows he will refuse to repeat his performance if ever the occasion again arises. Some time later, after Belfagor has possessed the daughter of the king of France, Gianmatteo is forced under pain of death to cure the girl since his reputation as an exorciser of spirits had by then spread over Europe. Belfagor refuses to leave the girl, and when all else fails, Gianmatteo devises a ruse that could not fail to frighten the poor devil out of his hiding place:

"Alas, Roderigo! It is your wife coming to reclaim you." It was a marvelous thing to behold what a shock the mere mention of his wife produced in Roderigo. It was so great that without thinking about whether it was possible or probable for her to be there, and without a word, he fled in terror, leaving the girl cured, for he preferred to return to hell to give an explanation of his actions rather than to live again with so many problems, dangers, and discomforts that marriage imposed upon him. And thus Belfagor, on his return to hell, testified to the evils that a wife brought into a household. And Gianmatteo, who knew more about such things than the devil, returned home happily.[15]

Gianmatteo's short exclamation contrasts with the long description of its effect upon Belfagor, underlining how frightened the devil was of his wife. Both Onesta, who had more pride than Lucifer, and Gianmatteo, who knew more than the devil, are more than a match for Belfagor; the contest between the humanized devil and these two earthly demons is an uneven one. In his skillful opening speech, Machiavelli revealed all the reader needs to know of a devil's character to explain Belfagor's problems on earth; Belfagor is susceptible to human passions and human failings even before he assumes a human form.

Machiavelli's literary masterpiece is his comedy, *Mandragola*.[16] Some critics have attempted to reduce the play to a political allegory where Callimaco represents Duke Lorenzo de' Medici, Lucrezia is Florence, and Nicia stands for the ill-fated *gonfaloniere* Soderini.[17] If such was Machiavelli's intention (and the idea is highly unlikely), it was certainly not noticed by his contemporaries, who considered the work a typical text, an exemplary model for comedy. From Machiavelli's day until the eighteenth century, the work was continuously read as a comedy, a work intended solely to delight the reader without necessarily containing political overtones or references to Machiavelli's political concepts.[18] Most modern critics read the play as a comedy of character rather than of plot; Luigi Russo believes, with good reason, that the characters in the play reflect the same tendency of portrait-painting, the same impulse to observe and describe human nature that occurred in Machiavelli's nonfictional works.[19] The traditional figures of the classical comedy are dimly recognizable in many of the characters (the parasite, the *senex*, the star-crossed lovers), but these figures are more than types. Each has a particular history; each is immersed in the society of the period so that the play has a contemporary, unconventional flavor.[20] As he did in the nonfictional works, Machiavelli presents his fictional characters totally defined from their initial appearance; it is their characterization rather than their personality that develops in the course of the play.[21]

Machiavelli's presentation of Lucrezia in the play is a good example of the way he normally portrays his characters. Although she is a pivotal figure in the work (her seduction constituting the plot), Lucrezia appears only four times on stage (3.10–11; 5.5–6). Since none of her appearances gives the audience an important insight into her personality, most of what the audience knows about her is contained in the remarks of others.[22] Yet, from only a few short remarks by several of his players, Machiavelli creates an extremely complex figure whose resemblance to the exemplum of chastity in Livy is only superficial.[23] The first description of Lucrezia is given by Callimaco and is a conventional, hyperbolic portrait of physical beauty with few important details; it is, furthermore, not a direct description of Lucrezia but a report of another's remarks:

He named Madonna Lucrezia, the wife of Nicia Calfucci, about whom he spoke so highly in terms of her beauty and her manners that all of us remained dumbfounded, and his praise caused me to have such a great desire to see her that, forgetting every other idea and no longer fearing whether Italy was at war or peaceful, I set out to see her: and after my arrival I found that the fame of Lucrezia's beauty is nothing when compared to her real beauty (something that rarely occurs), and I desire her so desperately that I am nearly out of my mind [1.1].[24]

Machiavelli does not emphasize the physical details of Lucrezia. Of more interest to him are her other qualities. All the reader knows of her physical appearance is a vague, general description of generic beauty that explains Callimaco's passion for her. Callimaco's own estimation of Lucrezia underlines an attribute of her personality that is even more striking than her beauty: "In the first place, her whole personality is against my designs upon her, for she is extremely virtuous and alien to thoughts of love: . . . so that there is not a bit of corruption in her" (1.1).[25] If Lucrezia's beauty is unrivaled in Florence, it is matched or even surpassed by her virtue, for she is a paragon of wifely fidelity and therefore presents a challenge to Callimaco, whose plan to seduce her resembles one of Borgia's military campaigns in its reliance upon cunning and deceit.

A more important commentary on Lucrezia's character — in fact, the key to an understanding of her actions in the play — is provided by the parasite Ligurio in a single penetrating remark. His evaluation is stated in essentially political terms: "a beautiful woman, wise, with good manners, and fit to govern a kingdom" (1.3).[26] Despite Messer Nicia's repeated denunciations of Lucrezia's foolishness, Machiavelli implies through Ligurio's remark that she possesses all those moral qualities that Machiavelli deemed necessary for the perfect ruler. It was probably this kind of comment that prompted some critics to suggest that the play is a political allegory. Callimaco's report on Lucrezia's reaction to his confession of love and her decision to accept him as her lover substantiates Ligurio's evaluation. Lucrezia possesses a typically Machiavellian awareness; she realizes that her husband's stupidity and the love of Callimaco have left her no rational alternative other than adultery, and as any good Machiavellian character might, she bends her actions to the *verità effettuale delle cose*:

After several sighs, she said: "Since your cunning, the stupidity of my husband, the unscrupulousness of my mother, and the evil nature of my confessor have brought me here to do that which I would never have done on my own, I wish to believe that it comes from some divine power which wishes me to act in this way, and since I am not capable of resisting heaven's wishes, I accept. And therefore I take you for lord, master, and guide: you must be everything for me — father and defender; and that which my husband wanted for one night, I want him to have forever" [5.4].[27]

Machiavelli admires Lucrezia's decision to accept Callimaco as her lover for the same reasons that he praises such figures as Cesare Borgia or Pope Julius II in his nonfictional works. Like these men, Lucrezia also avoids the contemptible middle road that Machiavelli usually found repulsive in political or private conduct. Ligurio's "political" evaluation of Lucrezia is therefore crucial to understanding her character and her eventual choice to accept Callimaco's suit after he was forced into her bedroom by her stupid husband in the hopes of satisfying his desire for a son. Russo suggests this (although he does not note the importance of Ligurio's remark) in his own evaluation of Lucrezia's decision, for he sees her as a figure characterized by *virtù* both first in her stubborn chastity and then in her willingness to completely accept Callimaco as her lover.[28] Although Lucrezia accepts Callimaco as her lover, this decision does not mean that she has undergone a change or a conversion. Blasucci's view that Lucrezia experiences a conversion is incorrect, though he qualifies his statement by defining it as an ethical conversion rather than an erotic one.[29] Radcliff-Umstead is even less aware of the meaning of Lucrezia's decision when he criticizes Machiavelli for "creating a rigid and fanatic character, ready to go from one extreme to the other."[30] There is no character development here. Lucrezia is initially defined as a person whose actions may vary but whose nature is constant in its avoidance of compromise. Her final decision only illuminates her nature. She is thus truly "fit to govern a kingdom" in Machiavelli's estimation.

The structure of *Mandragola* is based upon an external threat to Messer Nicia's family — the seduction of Lucrezia by Callimaco. In *Clizia*, the situation is reversed, for the play presents a family embroiled in an internal struggle because of the conflicting desires of its members. Nicomaco and his wife, Sofronia, disagree over the choice of a husband for their ward, Clizia. Since Nicomaco wants Clizia for himself, he supports Sofronia in her opposition to their son, Cleandro's, desire to marry Clizia. Nicomaco is the main figure of the play, since it is his love for Clizia that threatens to ruin the family's reputation and honor. Machiavelli based the work loosely upon Plautus' *Casina*, but *Clizia* is far from a simple imitation. Plautus's married couple represented two stock characters of Latin comedy, the *senex* and the "Xanthippe-type shrew." [31] Machiavelli's Nicomaco is a more sympathetic figure, for he is a good man whose senile passion for Clizia has radically, but only temporarily, altered his nature. Sofronia's opposition to his love for Clizia is not motivated by jealousy but by an honest desire to bring him back to his senses. Unlike Messer Nicia, whose blind stupidity is a constant source of mirth in *Mandragola*, Nicomaco is a more self-conscious character who understands that his love for Clizia is dangerous. Early in the play, he says: "Oh God, this old age brings all sorts of problems with it! But I am not too old yet to break a lance with Clizia. Yet, is it possible that I can be in love in this fashion?" (2.1).[32]

Nicomaco is presented to the audience in a masterful sketch delivered by Sofronia.[33] The longest description of one character by another in any of the comedies, her remarks fill an entire scene:

Anyone who knew Nicomaco a year ago and saw his habits now could not but be amazed at the great change that has occurred in him. Because he used to be serious, resolute, and respectable. He spent his time honorably. He woke up early in the morning, heard his mass, and attended to the day's provisions: then, if he had any business in town, at the market, or at the magistrates' office, he saw to that, and if not, he either talked about some serious topic with some citizens or retired to his desk where he balanced his accounts: then, he dined happily with his family, and after dinner talked with his son — giving him advice, helping him to know the ways of men, and teaching him how to live with exempla from the present and the past. Then he went out and passed the rest of the day either in business or in other serious and honest pursuits: in the evening, he was always home by dark, he stayed by the fire with us if it was winter, then he went into his study to review his affairs, and he later had a cheerful supper. His way of life was an example to everyone, and everyone was ashamed not to imitate him, and so things went — well ordered and happy [2.4].[34]

Before love altered his nature, Nicomaco was an admirable father, the perfect model of the bourgeois family man who even used the method Machiavelli practiced in his theoretical works — exempla from the past and the present — to instruct his son on human nature. But all of this changed with his passion for Clizia:

But since he has taken a fancy to this girl, he neglects his affairs, his farms are coming to ruin, and his commerce is falling apart. He's always yelling about something, though he doesn't know why, he comes in and out of the house a thousand times a day without knowing where he is going, he never returns to eat dinner or supper on time, and if you speak to him, he either doesn't answer or he answers in a way that shows he wasn't listening. The servants, seeing this, make fun of him, and his son has lost all respect for him; everyone does as they like, and they don't hesitate to follow his example. Thus, I am afraid that this poor house will be ruined if God does not come to our aid [2.4].[35]

This detailed portrait of Nicomaco presents two diametrically opposing views of his character at different points in time. Each of Nicomaco's former virtues becomes corrupted by his passion. The behavior of the model husband, the exemplary father, is sharply contrasted to his shameful conduct after he falls in love with Clizia by the phrase "But since," placed in the center of the sketch for emphasis.

Sofronia's attempts to save her family from ruin provide the comedy's plot. During the rest of the play, she attempts to restore order to the chaotic situation Nicomaco's senile love has created. Her attitude toward her husband as revealed by her description of him is important in understanding Nicomaco's character, for this portrait shows the audience that Nicomaco is not a fool like Messer Nicia but a good man gone astray. Even though Sofronia has good cause for anger, she strives only to rectify matters. Her affection for the "real" Nicomaco, the man she knows he really is (not the man he has become in the second half of the sketch) is apparent in her opening remarks. Her just assessment of Nicomaco's real nature explains why she succeeds in correcting his errors, since only a basically sound character could be cured of its mistakes. Sofronia substitutes one of her trusted male servants for Clizia on the night of Clizia's wedding to Pirro, Nicomaco's accomplice, and when Nicomaco replaces Pirro to enjoy Clizia's favors, he receives the beating his behavior has deserved. This *beffa* or trick was Sofronia's only means of bringing Nicomaco to his senses. When Nicomaco describes what occurred as he mistook the disguised servant for Clizia, his shame reveals how Sofronia's stratagem has caused him to regain his senses:

My friend, I don't know where to run, where to hide, or how to cover up the shame I have brought upon myself. I am disgraced for life without remedy, and I shall never be able to face my wife, children, relatives, or servants again. I was asking for it, and my wife pushed the matter along, and now I am done for [5.2].[36]

Nicomaco realizes that he has brought his misfortune upon himself; he repents of his senile love for Clizia and seeks his wife's pardon. The compassion Sofronia revealed in her earlier description of her husband moves her to forgive him if he will become his former self once more: "If you are willing to return to your former state and be that Nicomaco that you were a year ago, we shall all start over and this episode will be forgotten; and even if it does become known, it is not unusual for one to reform himself" (5.3).[37] In the original Italian, Sofronia's words to Nicomaco may be a humorous reference to one of Machiavelli's favorite theories explained in the *Discourses*, that states have to be purged of their corruption by a return to their first principles: "The means of renewing them, as I have said, is to bring them back to their former state. . . . And because in time the goodness of an institution is corrupted, it will of necessity ruin the body unless something intervenes to return it to its normal condition" (3.1).[38]

In like manner, Nicomaco had to be purged of his corrupting passion by a cruel trick before he could return to his former respectability. Like Lucrezia, Nicomaco only seems to change in the play. In reality, the apparent developments only illuminate his character, for his passion produces only a momentary deviation from his true nature as a model family man, husband, and merchant. In each comedy, Machiavelli skillfully uses the comments of other characters in sketching the portraits of these two individuals. After Ligurio's description of Lucrezia or Sofronia's portrait of Nicomaco, the audience has all the information it needs to understand the subsequent developments.

Machiavelli's portraits of Lucrezia and Nicomaco are drawn by remarks of other characters. In contrast to this usual method of presenting his fictional characters, Machiavelli presents Fra Timoteo in *Mandragola* through the friar's own soliloquies.[39] The priest does not enter the play until Act 3, scene 3, but after his first appearance, his portrait becomes a theme second only in importance to the seduction of Lucrezia. His initial appearance shows him performing the duties of his office as he discusses affairs with an anonymous woman. When she asks if he is sure that her husband is in purgatory, Timoteo replies immediately, "Without a doubt," but he assures her that only her continued devotion (in the form of monetary offerings) will ensure her spiritual happiness. Timoteo's desire to serve anyone who will pay him well is even more apparent as he greets Nicia and the notorious parasite Ligurio as *uomini da bene* (3.4). When Ligurio tricks Timoteo into assisting the plot against Lucrezia's virtue by persuading him first to agree to aid in a fictitious abortion, Fra Timoteo seems to be a stock character of medieval literature — the unworthy priest.

But Machiavelli's Fra Timoteo is more than just an unworthy priest, for scenes 3 and 4 of Act 3 only introduce him to the audience. His subsequent soliloquies (3.9; 4.6; 5.2; 5.3) and his "sermon" to Lucrezia (3.11) reveal that he is a complex character. His first soliloquy, delivered after he has been tricked into helping Ligurio and Nicia, shows his cunning:

I don't know who is fooling whom. That rascal Ligurio came to me with that first story to test me, so that if I refused to aid him in that first affair, he would have said nothing about the other in order not to reveal their plans, and the false pretext doesn't even concern them. It's true that I have been tricked; nevertheless this ruse can still be profitable to me. Messer Nicia and Callimaco are rich, and I should be able to get quite a bit out of both of them for different reasons; the affair must be kept secret, since that is as much in my interest as in their own. Come what may, I'll have no regrets [3.9].[40]

Timoteo's reference to his "temptation" by Ligurio underscores that fact that his idea of religion is not that of a pious Christian. The false story of a girl in need of an abortion is called a "test" or a "temptation" because it forced the priest to reveal his greed, but the true purpose of Ligurio's conversation (an even more outrageous proposal) is only viewed as an opportunity to make a profit. Timoteo has absolutely no regrets about being duped into the plot as long as there is money in it for him.

Timoteo's sermon to Lucrezia, meant to convince her that sleeping with a total stranger is no sin, is a masterful parody of pulpit rhetoric, what one critic calls "pre-Jesuitic casuistry":[41]

As far as your conscience is concerned, you should take this as a general rule, that where there is a certain good and an uncertain evil, the good should never be avoided for fear of the evil. Here we have a certain good — you will conceive and bear a child, producing a soul for Our Lord. The uncertain evil is that the man who sleeps with you after he takes the mandrake potion may die, but it is also possible that he won't die. But since there is some danger, it is best that Messer Nicia not run this risk. As for the act itself, whether or not it is a sin is foolish to discuss, for it is the will that sins, not the body; the true sin is to displease your husband (but you will be pleasing him) or to take pleasure in the act (but it displeases you). Besides this, in all things one must look to the result: the outcome of your act is to fill a seat in Paradise and to please your husband. The Bible says that the daughters of Lot, believing themselves to be alone in the world, lay with their father; and, because their intent was good they did not sin [3.11].[42]

Timoteo's specious logic in this mock sermon, his willingness to mistake the letter of the Christian religion for the spirit, is akin to the theology of an early Protestant sect which believed that if man should sin more, grace might abound. His final argument, the theory that the intention of an act determines its sinfulness, is so broad that it could justify any deed, no matter how evil. His final example of Lot's daughters is a perversion of the typical method of religious argument, an exemplum taken from the scriptures. The passage is a virtuoso performance of a man whose whole philosophy is that good intentions can justify anything.

Timoteo's second soliloquy reveals his complete lack of guilt or shame for his part in Ligurio's plot:

It is surely true what many people say, that bad company leads men to the gallows, and one can end just as badly being too credulous or good as one can being too evil. God knows that I never intended to hurt anyone, that I was in my cell saying my office and looking after my flock; then along comes this devil Ligurio, who first made me dip my finger into misconduct, then my arm, and then all of me, and I still don't know where it will end. But one thing consoles me — when a matter concerns many people, no one in particular can be blamed [4.6].[43]

Timoteo's description of himself as "too credulous or good" and of his co-conspirators as "bad company" is not meant to be humorous. He really believes that he is an innocent victim. But his own words betray him, for he admits that Ligurio only tempted him, only dipped his finger into the plot, as he puts it. His own greed, and not the influence of others

as he claims, is the cause of his complicity. The explanation
for Timoteo's feelings is given in another soliloquy:

So great was my desire to know how Callimaco and the others did
last night that I couldn't shut my eyes. I tried to pass the time in
various ways: I said matins, read one of the lives of the Fathers,
went into the church and lit a lamp that had burned out, and
changed the veil on the Madonna who works miracles. How many
times have I told these friars to keep it clean! And they wonder
why devotion declines. I remember when she had five hundred
marks of devotion around her, and today there are less than twenty;
this is our fault because we haven't maintained her reputation. . . .
Now nothing is done about it, and they marvel at the fact that the
devotion of the people is cold! Oh, how stupid these monks are!
[5.1].[44]

Timoteo's description of his daily tasks shows that his religion
is totally external, concerned with form alone and not with
ethical content. Because he equates religion with ritual, he
feels that these daily tasks satisfy all that God demands of
him. He therefore sees himself as a model priest, guiltless in
his complicity with Ligurio and Callimaco. Since he has convinced himself that his intentions are good ones, nothing he
does can constitute a sin. In his final soliloquy, he confesses
without shame that he uses the church as a place of business, a
brokerage that caters to the illicit desires of his parishioners.
After he has overheard Nicia's promise to pay him handsomely
for his part in the plot, Timoteo says:

I heard what he said about his success, and it pleased me, considering the stupidity of Messer Nicia; but the conclusion about my
reward pleased me the most. And since they must come to find
me, I won't stay here any longer but shall await them in the church,
where I can obtain the best price for my services [5.3].[45]

In these successive soliloquies, Machiavelli reveals Timoteo's
character completely. From the initial introduction of the

character (3.3–4) and his "sermon" to Lucrezia (3.9), the audience sees Timoteo's character through his actions. In the soliloquies, the friar's own words reveal why he acts as he does. The result is the sketch of a perfect rascal, a priest who sins without remorse and constantly proclaims his innocence. It is a portrait superior to any that Machiavelli created in his other literary works, a sketch of a more complex character than we have seen in the historical works.

Critics have traditionally claimed that Machiavelli separated public or political morality from private ethics in his works, but in those works which treat private life, there is no independent moral norm. The world of *Belfagor, Clizia,* and *Mandragola* is the same world that produced Borgia, Pope Julius II, and Castruccio, a world "characterized by the rule of will and desire (*la voglia e il desiderio*) using force (*forza*) and fraud (*fraude*) as their means of acquiring their ever-changing objects of desire." [46] It is not surprising that Lucrezia's personality should be defined by Ligurio in essentially political terms or that Nicomaco's "cure" should remind us of Machiavelli's belief that corruption can only be removed by returning to first principles. This should not obscure the fact that these are primarily literary works; their "political" aspects serve only to aid Machiavelli in his portraits of the characters. In both his treatment of Lucrezia, where Machiavelli develops an astute observation based upon a crucial political metaphor, and in the opening speech of *Belfagor,* where a nonintentional revelation of character by Pluto presents vital information concerning the nature of hell's inhabitats which explains Belfagor's difficulties on earth, Machiavelli has used the words of his characters to present indirectly elements of their personalities. The two sketches of. Nicomaco and Timoteo are even more elaborate, the first using the more common method of employing the comments of other players to sketch a character, the second using the character's own soliloquies to lay bare his inner nature.

The literary qualities of Machiavelli's private letters have already been mentioned. One of these, for example, describes the misadventures of a Florentine homosexual, Giuliano Brancacci, in such a way as to make it a worthy successor to the ribald tradition of Boccaccio.[47] An equally hilarious letter is more important for our study of the art of portraiture, since it contains a grotesque sketch of a hideous prostitute. The letter is written to Luigi Guicciardini, the brother of the more famous Francesco, and is dated 8 December 1509. Machiavelli claims the letter is a true account of one of his adventures, but it is more probable that the story is fictitious, something akin to the *vituperium* of the medieval goliardic poets or the Italian *poeti giocosi*.[48] Machiavelli is introduced to the prostitute by an old bawd who uses a clever euphemism to sell her wares:

I came across an old woman who washed my shirts; her house is more than half underground, and the only light comes in from the door. I was passing by there one day and she recognized me, making a great show of her welcome, and she said that, if I wanted to do so, she could show me some beautiful shirts to see if I wanted to buy them. Whereupon, I believed her — young innocent that I am — and when I was inside I saw dimly a woman hiding in a corner who was pretending to be bashful with a towel over her head and face. The old bawd took my by the hand and led me to the woman, saying: "This is the shirt that I want to sell, but I want you to try it on first and pay later." [49]

Although Machiavelli pretends he is a novice in such matters, he nevertheless agrees to sample the "merchandise" the bawd is selling.

After satisfying his lust, Machiavelli picks up a brand from the fire to get a better look at the prostitute and soon learns why the room was dark and why she pretended to be shy. What follows is the single instance of a detailed physical description in all of Machiavelli's works:

My God! The woman was so ugly that I almost fell dead to the ground. The first thing I noticed was a tuft of hair, half white and half black, and although the top of her head was bald — that allowed you to see several lice taking a stroll — nevertheless a few hairs mingled with the whiskers that grew down to her eyelashes; and on top of her small, wrinkled head there was a scar-burn which made her look as if she had been branded at the market; her eyebrows were full of nits; one eye looked down, the other up, and one was larger than the other. Her tear ducts were full of mucus and her eyelashes plucked; her nose was twisted into a funny shape, the nostrils were full of snot, and one of them was half cut off; her mouth was similar to Lorenzo de' Medici's, but was twisted on one side and drooled a bit, since she had no teeth to keep her saliva in her mouth; her upper lip was covered with a thin but rather long beard; her chin was long and sharp, pointed up, and from it hung a bit of skin that dangled to her Adam's apple. As I stood there amazed at this monster, she noticed my surprise and tried to say: "What is the trouble, sir?"; but she could not since she was a stutterer; . . . This was such a shock to my stomach that, not being to bear it, it heaved so much that I vomited upon her.[50]

We have already seen that Machiavelli only attempts physical description when it complements his evaluation of the moral or intellectual qualities of a character. In the portraits of the Duke of Athens, Castruccio Castracani, or Cosimo de' Medici, physical details were symbolic of other more important qualities. Only once, in this private letter, does Machiavelli allow his descriptive skill full expression in the depiction of physical details. The result is this grotesque masterpiece, the very essence of ugliness. The things Machiavelli observes — the lice strolling on the prostitute's brow or the similarity of her mouth to that of Lorenzo de' Medici — are no more intended to communicate a true picture than were the physical details of other portraits.[51] The grotesque quality of this sketch is created by the description of a woman's face in such a manner that it is no longer recognizable as such.

VIII *The Portrait of the Artist*

As is evident from an examination of the
historical works, Machiavelli only rarely reveals information
about himself in his narrative. While his sharp mind and
learning are everywhere apparent, little can be discovered
about the man himself. For example, all he reveals of his
private life in the diplomatic correspondence is his constant
complaint about Florence's stinginess in paying his salary and
traveling expenses while he is undertaking important missions
for the city. Machiavelli does inject himself into the early
essay on Borgia's actions at Sinigaglia, making it appear that it
was his arrival from Florence with aid that caused Borgia
to regain his courage, thereafter destroying the Magione conspirators. Machiavelli's recasting of this event to include himself seems to be a product of his intense desire to be near the
center of political power, to forget his own position as a
second-rank diplomatic ambassador. Occasionally, the reader
can see his fierce Florentine pride in conversations with men
of high rank, for Machiavelli is generally not afraid to speak
his own mind. His retort to Cardinal d'Amboise as reported
in *The Prince* is the best example of this bluntness.

For a fuller evaluation of Machiavelli's character as
reflected in his writings, for a portrait of the artist, one must
turn to his private letters and scattered passages in the literary
works. Critics have most often stressed a single aspect of this
self-portrait, Machiavelli's bitterness in exile, his so-called

"tragic" fate. For example, he ends the dedication to *The Prince* with the following statement to Lorenzo de' Medici: "And should Your Highness look down from the summit of your exalted position toward this lowly spot, you will know the great and unmerited sufferings I bear because of a cruel fate." [1] The same sense of injustice is evident in the prolog to *Mandragola*:

> And if this material seems unworthy,
> because it is too frivolous,
> of a man who wishes to appear wise and serious,
> excuse him for it, since he tries
> with these little trifles
> to make his time less harsh,
> for he does not have anywhere else
> to turn himself:
> because he has been forbidden
> to show his mettle in other affairs,
> there being no reward for his labors. [2]

This view of a "victimized" Machiavelli, of a man crushed by ill-fortune, is only one aspect of the manner in which he represented himself in his works, however. Machiavelli intended that his correspondence should reveal more to posterity than just a few elements of his personality.

Giorgio Bàrberi Squarotti has seized upon the portions of Machiavelli's correspondence that reflect the so-called "tragic" side of his life and has erected an elaborate theory to explain Machiavelli's manner of viewing the world. [3] He sees a rigid separation between the sublime and the comic style in Machiavelli's works (especially in the letters), a stylistic tendency which reveals the workings of the man's mind and his method of representing reality. Bàrberi Squarotti believes that the "sublime" style is used only to treat important theoretical questions, while the "comic" style deals with practice, concrete action, life in the world. This attitude is supposed to reflect the traditional concept of separation of stylistic levels on the basis of subject matter which was born in classical literature and which was continued by most neo-classical literary movements. There is no doubt that such a theory of levels of style was common in the Italian Renaissance, but it is unlikely that Machiavelli followed such a theory in his works.

Bàrberi Squarotti cites several important private letters as evidence for his claim that Machiavelli's works demonstrate this theory of rigid separation of stylistic levels and content. He believes that the letter of 9 April 1513, addressed to Francesco Vettori, wherein Machiavelli writes of his burning impulse to speak of politics signifies a radical division between the sublime subject of politics and the more mundane topics of daily life.[4] In that letter Machiavelli had declared:

And yet, if I could talk to you, you could not keep me from filling my brain with castles in Spain, for Fortune has decreed that since I cannot talk about the silk or wool business or of profits and losses, it suits me to discuss politics, and I have to discuss that or remain silent.[5]

Machiavelli's most famous letter is that of 10 December 1513, also addressed to Francesco Vettori, in which he describes his daily activity after his exile and the genesis of *The Prince*. After spending the day snaring birds, reading Dante, Petrarch, or other poets, and meeting a few disagreeable people in the local tavern, Machiavelli returns home in the evening:

When evening comes, I return to my home, and I go into my study; and on the threshold, I take off my street clothes which are covered with mud and mire, and I put on regal and curial robes; and dressed in a more appropriate manner I enter into the old courts of the ancients and am welcomed by them kindly, and there I taste the food that alone is mine, and for which I was born; and there I am not ashamed to speak to them, to ask them the reasons for their actions; and they, in their humanity, answer me; . . . I have noted down what I have learned from their conversation, and I composed a little work, *De principatibus*.[6]

Bàrberi Squarotti sees in this letter the essence of Machiavelli's separation of the sublime and the comic, the world of intellectual contemplation and the world of reality. He also claims to find the same neat separation of style and content in letters describing the grotesque prostitute (8 December 1509), Giuliano Brancacci's homosexual escapades (25 February 1514), and Machiavelli's practical jokes at the expense of the Carpi friars (17–19 March 1521). For this critic, the link between these two levels of reality is always the tragic figure of Machiavelli, the hero who narrates and who constitutes the point of reference for all of these letters.[7]

Bàrberi Squarotti is correct in stressing the importance of the two letters from which I have quoted at length; Machiavelli's expressed preference for discussions of political matters over business and the changing of his "dirty" clothes for "regal and curial garments" obviously reflect his partiality for the study of the ancients to his life in exile from political activity. But the assertion that these letters prove the existence of a neo-classical stylistic division between the "comic" or low style and the "sublime" or tragic style is a distortion of Machiavelli's works and his expressed intentions. In essence, this critic takes the scattered references to a tragic or victimized Machiavelli — admittedly present in his works — and makes this autobiographical element a key to the interpretation of Machiavelli's mode of thought. Some objections to this line of interpretation have already been mentioned in chapters on the comedies and *Belfagor*, as well as those discussing *The Prince* and the *Discourses*, but Bàrberi Squarotti's discussion of the private letters has a stronger appeal since it is partially based upon textual evidence. Machiavelli's references to his fate often show his bitterness, but they do not provide a sufficient basis for the argument that he practiced a neo-classical separation of styles or topics. Moreover, the letters Bàrberi Squarotti chooses to examine are naturally one-sided, since they are written shortly after Machiavelli's fall from power and before he had time to adjust to his change of fortune. In fact, though Bàrberi Squarotti accuses other critics of noticing only Machiavelli's content, he too confuses the "tragic" content of the letters with their style and never really demonstrates in what ways the "comic" and the "sublime" Machiavelli differ.

Paul O. Kristeller has noted that the Renaissance private letter, and especially those written by men who worked in the Florentine Chancellery, was "not merely a vehicle of personal communication; it was intended from the beginning as a literary composition to be copied and read." [8] Machiavelli was no exception, and it is significant that in one of his letters dated 31 January 1515 (which Bàrberi Squarotti ignores), he discusses his view of how comic and serious matters should be represented in his letters:

Whoever might see our letters, my dear friend, and might note their diversity would be very amazed, for at one point he would think that we were very serious men, involved in great matters, and that we never entertained a thought that was not honest and lofty. But then, turning the page, he would find that these same serious men were frivolous, inconstant, lustful, and occupied with trifles. This manner of ours, although to some it may be disgraceful, seems laudable to me, because we imitate nature, which itself is various, and whoever imitates nature cannot be blamed. And although we usually do not always show this variety in every letter, this time I am going to do it in one, as you will see if you read the other side. Spit.[9]

Machiavelli clearly rejects any facile separation of styles or subject matter here. He sees life as an organic whole, a unity of both the trivial and the tragic, the comic and the serious. He defends his mixture of so-called comic and sublime elements in his letters by arguing that the imitation of nature demands both great matters (*cose grandi*) and trifles (*cose vane*). Far from viewing reality through rigidly distinct categories derived, as Bàrberi Squarotti believes, from classical practice, Machiavelli uses an essentially classical argument — the imitation of nature as the artist's goal — to defend his own mixture of styles and topics.

This same letter is a reply to a letter from Francesco Vettori, dated 16 January 1515.[10] In it, Vettori had declared in the most serious terms that copulation was man's greatest pleasure: "I don't know anything more fun to think about or to do than fornication. Men can philosophize about it all they wish, but that's the pure truth, as many realize but few will admit." [11] Machiavelli had earlier told Vettori in a letter dated 3 August 1514, that he had turned away from all thought of politics and had given himself to dreaming about love: "I have given up all thoughts about grand and serious affairs; reading about the ancients or arguing about modern affairs no longer pleases me; everything has given place to amorous conversations, for which I thank Venus and the whole Cyprian isle." [12] Bàrberi Squarotti saw the statement in the letter of 9 August 1513 — "it suits me to discuss politics, and I have to discuss that or remain silent" — as the key to the working of Machiavelli's mind. But it is misleading to separate this letter, where politics is defined as Machiavelli's sole interest, from that of 3 August 1514, where he drops the so-called "sublime" topic of politics for the "comic" subject of love. As he so clearly underlines in the reference to the mixture of topics in his letters, each subject is part of his vision of reality, his imitation of nature. Though his subject may change, his style remains the same.

Even the structure of the letter of 31 January 1515 renders his theoretical statement that mimesis involves a mixture of *cose grandi* and *cose vane*. Machiavelli begins his answer to Vettori's discussion of love with an original sonnet on the subject, describing the effects of Cupid on his own life. He then quotes a literary passage that deals with love, Ovid's *Metamorphoses* (1.504–507). Having given two literary definitions of his topic, he pauses and considers the imitation of nature in his private letters, setting forth the opinion cited previously. Almost puckishly, he ends the discussion with the abrupt phrase "Spurgatevi," directing Vettori to "spit" or "purge himself" of one subject so that he can move to the other on the reverse side of the letter. From love, he then moves to a consideration of political matters, treating Cesare Borgia and Giuliano de' Medici (the brother of Pope Leo X) in the same familiar manner that he earlier used to discuss love. Again, a literary illusion — this time from Pulci's *Morgante* (1.38, 7–8) — is cited from memory to embellish his treatment. Far from separating the subjects of love and politics by a shift in style and tone, he treats both in the same manner. He makes a conscious effort to underline his purpose by the centrally placed paragraph which justifies his presentation on the grounds that such a mixture would best imitate nature's variety. It is not inappropriate to recall Dante's treatment of the sublime and comic styles that were rigidly separated in classical literature. Machiavelli's expressed desire to imitate nature by reflecting all its variety is not unlike Dante's practice. As Erich Auerbach describes it, "the themes which the Comedy introduces represent a mixture of sublimity and triviality which, measured by the standards of antiquity, is monstrous . . . Dante knows no limits in describing with meticulous care and directness things which are humdrum, grotesque, or repulsive." [13] Machiavelli's epistolary style never intended to reach the heights of Dante's epic, but it does, by his own testimony, attempt to represent a multifaceted reality in a way that recalls Dante's practice. If there is a stylistic precedent for Machiavelli's "imitation of nature," it is not a classical one but rather the example of Dante, whom Machiavelli knew by heart. [14]

The portrait Machiavelli paints of himself in his letters and other works goes far beyond the tragic figure of an embittered politician exiled from his only concern in life. The Machiavelli revealed is a complex individual with a multifaceted personality. Behind the remarks he makes about himself, even the most serious, there is the hint that he never took himself too seriously. Although he was a learned man, one of his letters parodies such erudition in his own comedies. Francesco Guicciardini wrote to Machiavelli, requesting the explanation for two colloquial expressions in the *Mandragola* — "fare a' sassi pe' forni" (2.4) and "come disse la botta all'erpice" (3.6) — but Machiavelli treated his request in a comic manner, apparently feeling that it was humorous for a Florentine nobleman to request information on Florentine expressions.[15] Instead of giving Guicciardini the explanation he requested, Machiavelli satirized his own learning in his reply (16–20 October 1525): "As for the toad and the harrow, this certainly calls for serious consideration. And truly I have, like Fra Timoteo, paged through many books in order to find the original citation, and finally I found something in Burchiello which does a lot for me." [16] The reference to Burchiello is completely gratuitous, having nothing to do with the proverbial expression under examination. Machiavelli's statement that the passage "does a lot for him" does not, of course, explain its source or meaning. He teases Guicciardini even further by claiming that Burchiello found the reference to the *erpice* (harrow) in the second Decade of Livy, a work that has never been recovered by modern bibliophiles. He ends the letter by telling Guicciardini to let him know if he still has any questions: "That is all of any relevance that I have found, and if your lordship still has any questions, let me know." [17]

The same playfully irreverent attitude is also present in *A Dialogue on Language* (circa 1514).[18] In this short treatise, Machiavelli argues that Dante wrote Tuscan rather than a hybrid language made of common elements of all Italian dialects or a language of the court: "There is no language which one can call common to Italy or a courtly language, since all those that may be so called have their basis in the works of Florentine writers and in the Florentine language." [19] Machiavelli's linguistic theories are irrelevant to our discussion, but the work also contains a brilliant debate between Machiavelli and the poet Dante. After an initial theoretical discussion of the *questione della lingua*, Machiavelli decides that he is tired of the abstract and wishes to get down to cases with Dante: "If what I say is true (and it certainly is), I should like to call Dante to show me his poem: . . . But I should like to have a little chat with Dante, and in order to avoid 'he said' and 'I replied,' I shall indicate the speakers." [20] This "little chat" with Dante becomes a comic debate as Machiavelli uses Dante's own poem to prove to the poet that he wrote in Florentine. Machiavelli finally assumes a magisterial tone and admonishes Dante as if he were a mischievous school boy, warning him to mend his ways: "Dante, my friend, I want you to mend your ways and consider more carefully the Florentine tongue and your own work." [21] Since, as Ridolfi notes,[22] Machiavelli has the advantage of being both plaintiff and judge in this debate, he is able to award himself the victory in the argument without difficulty: "When Dante had listened to these remarks, he confessed that I was correct and went away; and I was very pleased about it, for it appeared to me that I had set him straight." [23] Although Machiavelli admired Dante above all other poets, imitated his poetry in his own verse, and constantly quoted him from memory in his letters, he wore his learning lightly and was able to poke fun at his idols just as he had at himself. Without the interjection of Machiavelli's own personality into this treatise, it might have become as dry as many other documents dealing with the *questione della lingua*. By bringing himself into the picture, he created a humorous debate which still rewards the reader's attention.

Machiavelli's habitual manner of mixing serious matters with comical ones accurately to reflect the variety present in nature is also apparent in several sonnets he sent to Giuliano de' Medici, the ruler of the city after the fall of the Florentine

Republic. After being tortured with six turns of the rack (since he was part of the ousted republican leadership), Machiavelli sent a humorous sonnet to Giuliano, his jailer:

> Giuliano, I have a set of irons on my legs
> and six turns of the rack on my shoulders:
> I do not intend to tell you my other miseries,
> since such is the manner in which they treat poets!
> These walls seem to breed lice
> so swollen that they look like butterflies,
> and there was never a stench at Roncesvalles
> or in Sardinia among those groves
> as in my delicate little hotel.[24]

In another sonnet sent to Giuliano along with a gift of a few thrushes he caught on his farm at Sant'Andrea after his release from prison, he says: "Giuliano, I am sending you some thrushes, / not because this gift is good or fine, / but because for a moment of poor Machiavelli / Your Magnificence may recall." [25] This poem begins with a note of bitterness and resentment over his years of service in the Florentine Chancellery that now go unrewarded, but this feeling is dissolved by Machiavelli's corrosive humor. He goes on to say that if there are any backbiters around Giuliano (any courtiers who would criticize Machiavelli), let them eat the birds so that they will cease biting him. It does not matter if the birds are thin, for he too is thin from their attacks: "I would answer such complaints / saying that I am thin, even I, as my enemies are aware, / and yet they get some good mouthfuls off me." [26]

Several portraits and busts of Machiavelli exist, the best of which is perhaps a portrait by Santi di Tito which hangs in the Palazzo Vecchio in Florence. Most of these works show Machiavelli's thin, compressed lips bearing an ironic smile.[27] Such a pose is typical of the man one sees behind the letters and the few glimpses of the author that the narrator permits in the historical and literary works. Pirandello once described Machiavelli as the perfect *umorista*, a man whose personality incarnated his famous *sentimento del contrario:* "Few minds were as disposed as his to the understanding of contrasts, to the reception, in a profound manner, of the impression of life's incongruousness." [28] The observation is a cogent one, for even in the worst of times in prison or in political exile, Machiavelli constantly saw more than just this gloomy side of his situation and represented not only his misfortunes but also the humor he saw in them. No episode in Machiavelli's life better demonstrates his sense of the incongruousness of life, his ability to smile in the worst of times, than his mission to the Franciscans in May of 1521, which is the subject of several letters Machiavelli and Francesco Guicciardini exchanged. After years of exile from political affairs, Machiavelli had finally obtained a new commission for the Medici rulers of Florence, a relatively minor mission for the Medici to the Chapter General of the Minor Friars being held at Carpi. Besides this task, he had also agreed to help the Consuls of the Wool Guild find a Lenten preacher. Considering Machiavelli's former place in the Chancellery, his own sense of self-importance, and his burning desire to regain a position of political influence, such a mission seems almost to have been a cruel joke perpetrated by the Medici.

However, Machiavelli was able to see the humorous aspect of his job and turned the whole event into a source of mirth. After Guicciardini had remarked in a letter of 17 May 1521 that sending Machiavelli to pick a preacher was much like sending a notorious Florentine sodomite to choose a beautiful wife for another man, Machiavelli replied that he was willing to undertake the mission, but that he intended to pick a preacher to his own special tastes:

When your letter arrived, I was on the privy thinking about the vanities of this world, and especially about how to find a preacher after my own tastes for Florence, one that would suit me alone, for in this I want to be as stubborn as in my ideas on other affairs. . . .

It is true that I differ with my fellow citizens in this as well as in other matters, for they want a preacher to show them the way to Paradise, and I want to find one that will show them how to go to the devil; they want a man who is serious and prudent, and I want one who is madder than Pozzo, more mercurial than brother Girolamo, and more hypocritical than brother Alberto, for it appears to me a fine thing, and one worthy of our times, that we see that which we have experienced in many priests all in one man; because I believe that the true way of going to Paradise is to learn the way to hell in order to avoid it.[29]

The first sentence of this marvelous passage itself combines serious and comic elements; we can almost see Machiavelli's smile as he informs Guicciardini that he was on the privy, thinking about the world's deep problems when his letter arrived. Instead of lamenting his fall from a position of authority in the Chancellery as an ambassador to the crowned heads of Europe to a lowly messenger boy at a gathering of motley friars, Machiavelli immediately seizes upon the comic possibilities of his mission to what Guicciardini had contemptuously called *la Repubblica de' Zoccholi*.[30] To improve the quality of his meals and lodging and to have a hearty laugh at the friars' expense, he persuaded Guicciardini to send him daily messengers who would make it appear to the friars that much important business of state was being transacted between Machiavelli and Guicciardini, the governor of the province. Guicciardini obliged, and the resulting letters are full of their laughter over the effect of the messengers upon the gullible friars. In the midst of such a comedy of errors, it was significantly Guicciardini, and not Machiavelli, who returned to serious matters and lamented Machiavelli's ill fortune to be reduced so low from his former station in life. In a letter dated 18 May 1521, Guicciardini wrote:

My dear Machiavelli. When I read your credentials as Ambassador of the Republic to the friars and consider how many kings, dukes, and princes you have negotiated with at other times, I cannot but recall Lysander who, after so many victories and triumphs, was given the task of passing out meat to the very soldiers he had so gloriously commanded; and I say: Only the faces and the outside appearances of men change, but the same events recur, and nothing happens which has not occurred before. But since the names and appearances of events change, only wise men recognize them.[31]

Such was Machiavelli's mission to Carpi. Ridolfi rightly sees this mission as symbolic of the whole of the man's life, for although Machiavelli's journey to Carpi brought him no credit with his Medici employers, "he gained esteem with posterity for having . . . put on a cheerful countenance and won honour with his brilliant letters even in times of adversity." [32]

IX   *The Concept of Character in Machiavelli's Prose*

Modern readers have a concept of character in narrative which has been aptly described as "hopelessly novel-centered." [1] Consequently, the reader's first impression of Machiavelli's nonfictional characters is their relative psychological simplicity. None of these figures is the kind of complex individual the modern reader has come to expect from long exposure to the novel, a genre that commonly stresses both character development and varying degrees of introspective analysis. Only in the portrait of the Duke of Athens do we feel we have been granted a glimpse into the intimate workings of a character's mind. Machiavelli's remark that Lorenzo de' Medici seemed to be composed of "two different persons" reveals his reluctance or inability to deal with complex, and therefore conflicting, personality traits in his nonfictional characters. A partial explanation is doubtless that Machiavelli's protagonists are part of a larger argument which limits his freedom of expression. Contained in what are essentially political or historical works, his portraits are designed to complement his arguments and to make them more convincing. He viewed history as a genre which should both please and instruct, but he would never have intended that his readers receive only entertainment from the character sketches he created. The fact that Machiavelli fails to depict individuals of great psychological complexity does not, however, justify the assertion that his protagonists in *The History of Florence* (or in his other works, for that matter) are allegorical types. Comparing Machiavelli's prose works to the modern novel which often specializes in introspective analysis of its characters is, of course, unfair. Machiavelli was not writing novels; he was using historical figures within a larger framework of theoretical discourse. While the individuals in his nonfictional works never display a "modern" complexity, they remain fascinating individuals through Machiavelli's skillful presentation. His favorite technique is the examination of a single personality trait to represent the inner qualities of an important historical individual. To this end, he uses all his talent to embellish his portraits to make of them more than hollow abstractions. The examination of a character's "nature" was always his initial concern, but he soon discovered that this limited subject was insufficient to express his literary impulse. Thus, in *The Prince* and the *Discourses,* he goes beyond his diplomatic and minor writings to portray symbolic individuals through their actions, using this more dynamic method to reveal their inner qualities. The sketches in *The History of Florence,* like those in these two theoretical works, also employ a man's actions to illustrate his moral or intellectual qualities, but the summary *elogium* Machiavelli uses in many of these sketches is a stylistic addition which he began in his fictional biography of his archetypal hero, Castruccio Castracani. Witty remarks, dying words, summary judgments, and symbolic physical details are all used in the *elogium,* which is itself often constructed upon rhetorical devices that reinforce Machiavelli's judgments. Machiavelli's use of such symbolic physical details in his descriptions is an innovation in Renaissance historical narrative; it is a stylistic trait completely absent in the narratives of earlier humanist historians such as Bruni or Bracciolini.[2]

The fact that Machiavelli's characters are part of an argument only partially explains their so-called simplicity, their lack of depth, however. Machiavelli's nonfictional works must be read in their proper context, that of classical history, biography, or epic, for one to comprehend why more fully developed characters were not considered necessary to such works. Ancient writers viewed history and biography as strictly separate genres. Plutarch, for instance, stated unequivocally that his work was a biography and not history.[3] Classical history usually described in detail the actions of its characters, while biography was more concerned with what kinds of persons its characters were. As a result, biography did not usually attempt a comprehensive analysis of a man's actions but stressed only those deeds and anecdotes which helped to uncover his personality.[4] Machiavelli's portraits are thus closer to classical biography than to history with one important caveat: Machiavelli typically employs what a person *does* to reflect what kind of person he *is*, relying more upon political actions than anecdotes to uncover his personality. His character sketches thus combine elements of both classical genres. Machiavelli must have been aware of his penchant for biography when in his closing remarks in *The History of Florence* on Cosimo de' Medici he apologized for using a style more appropriate to the description of the lives of princes than to the writing of history.

When Machiavelli's nonfictional works are read against their proper classical background, the modern reader is also no longer surprised that his protagonists rarely develop or change their natures in the course of a portrait. On the contrary, the narrative usually reveals their latent traits as initially defined by the narrator. The portrayal of character development is a relatively recent phenomenon in the history of narrative prose.[5] In the works of Machiavelli, as well as in those of many classical historians and biographers, a character is conceived as a complete entity from the beginning of the narrative; what develops or unfolds in the course of the work is not a development of the character itself but of the characterization.[6] The presentation of character in the classical epic, another genre concerned with the heroic life and exemplary deeds, has much in common with that in prose narrative. Homer's Achilles in his *Iliad*, for instance, is a brilliant portrait which is neither inclusive nor detailed. The man is presented by the narrator to the readers in terms of only one aspect of his character — the emotion of anger.[7]

The greatest of Machiavelli's portraits is the sketch of Castruccio Castracani because of its length, its stylistic features (many of which are repeated in *The History of Florence*), and its literary structure as an archetypal biography. But each of Machiavelli's other works would be much less interesting as literature without the popes, the Borgias, the Medicis, the heroes and the villains who are liberally sprinkled throughout them all. For Machiavelli, history was far from a subject of academic study. Past events were a living part of the present, and they revealed lessons for the future. His decision to make artistic character sketches such an integral part of his prose works was a happy one, for it added the literary touch to works which, without such portraits, would have become dry treatises like his *Art of War*. *The Art of War*, commonly regarded as the least interesting of Machiavelli's major works, is completely devoid of striking literary portraits. Without his attention to the art of portraiture, Machiavelli's political ideas might have been just as revolutionary, but they would scarcely have had the same impact upon generations of fascinated readers. Like the figures in the works of Livy or Plutarch who were proposed by their creators as exemplary models which were followed by civilized Europeans for centuries, Machiavelli's characters were meant to be practical guides, illustrations of certain fixed principles in human nature. It is in this sense that his nonfictional works represent a rebirth of the classical concept of the heroic character in modern prose narrative. Although his protagonists are uncomplicated or unidimensional, this feature subtracts nothing from their literary merits anymore than it diminishes the effectiveness of the protagonists of Homer, Livy, or Plutarch.

My examination of selected figures from Machiavelli's literary works reveals certain similarities between his fictional and nonfictional characters. As demonstrated in the cases of Belfagor, Lucrezia, or Nicomaco, Machiavelli rarely deals with character development in his comedies. His subjects are initially defined by their particular attributes, and the resulting narrative simply illuminates their personalities. In both his historical and fictional sketches, it is the characterization — not the character — that develops, and the emphasis is always upon the moral or intellectual traits of these personalities. Both groups have relatively simple traits; they are usually shown to have a major defining quality or several complementary traits which rarely conflict. Physical description is minimal, yet when present, it enhances more important aspects of an individual. All we know of Lucrezia's appearance, for example, is that she is extremely beautiful. The important exception to this general rule in the literary works is the grotesque portrait of a prostitute. These common features enable us to define such characterization as a typical aspect of Machiavelli's works, historical, political, and literary. The major difference between these two general groups of characters is generic. Even though the figures I examined in the first six chapters must be considered "literary" characters because of the stylized method of their presentation, they were basically historical individuals, part of a serious, didactic argument. In contrast to these exempla, Machiavelli presents fictional characters within a comic framework.

A proper examination of Machiavelli's correspondence would constitute a separate study. My brief treatment of the portrait of the artist in Machiavelli's letters and selected works is sufficient to reveal some major differences between Machiavelli's historical or literary characters and his own self-portrait. Machiavelli's characters, even the most intriguing, are rarely psychologically complex individuals. In contrast to the relative simplicity of his characters, the author appears to be an extremely complex individual. One finds glimpses of a large number of differing opinions, moods, and attitudes in his letters, all of them infinitely more subtle than any of his characters. At times, he shows himself in an almost tragic light, a figure embittered by his ill fortune. This more serious aspect of his personality produced some of his great letters, notably his description of how he wrote *The Prince* after evening discussions with the ancients, or how his mind refused to consider anything but politics. But, behind his seriousness always remains the ironic smile of the humorist in Pirandello's sense. Machiavelli often forgot his own personal problems, or more accurately, he turned his despair into masterpieces of comedy as in the description of his encounter with a grotesque prostitute or of his practical joke at Carpi. Conflicting, even contradictory, aspects of his personality abound in the self-portrait one can construct from his letters. At one moment, he rejects everything but the discussion of political questions; in another mood, he leaves the *antiche cose* behind and turns exclusively to the sweeter subject of love. He rarely notes such conflicting moods in his literary portraits, and when he does notice them, as in his sketch of Lorenzo de' Medici, they seem to puzzle him. Machiavelli certainly expected that his private letters would be read by posterity, although he did not rewrite and polish them to the same degree as, for example, Petrarch did. Machiavelli wanted his letters to present not just a statically defined literary figure but a man whose many and diverse emotions, moods, opinions, and goals were accurately portrayed as they actually occurred with a mixture of the serious and the humorous, the trivial and the tragic. Attempting to trace character development in a collection of private letters may be inappropriate, but there is, nevertheless, a kind of development in the letters read as a whole. It is a maturing process, Machiavelli's gradual acceptance of ill fortune and his conscious attempt to make the best of it. Most often, Machiavelli uses laughter as a defense against a cruel world, turning misfortune into comedy. His references to himself in his letters and his other works paint the portrait of a learned, psychologically deep, and warmly human Renaissance man.

Far removed from the cynical, diabolic figure that the legend of Machiavellianism inspired to distort his true character for centuries, Niccolò Machiavelli embodied the best aspects of Renaissance culture. He was as enthusiastic a humanist as Petrarch, though he was less learned and less concerned with the appreciation of literature on its artistic merits alone. As intelligent and sharp-witted as Montaigne (and perhaps equally well-read), his vision was clearest when it dealt with the practical world of politics rather than the inner world of the psyche. Like many of the so-called "pagans" of his times, he composed a deeply religious work, *An Exhortation to Penitence*, and ended it, appropriately enough for a man who loved Italian poetry, with a line from Petrarch about the world's vanity.[8] He felt the many diverse elements that composed his personality, perhaps more clearly than he noted such diversity in his characters. He once composed a *strambotto* intended to reflect his innermost feelings, using the characteristic Petrarchan antitheses that the European Renaissance saw as the most effective vehicle for poetic introspection and for rendering the psychological conflicts that pensive men have always noted in their own hearts.[9]

Within the larger and darker legend of Machiavelli that grew up after his death, there is a curious story of a dream he reported on his deathbed to his friends. Most biographers have called this tale apocryphal, an anecdote fabricated by Machiavelli's detractors to make him appear in a bad light to posterity.[10] More perceptively, however, Machiavelli's latest biographer believes that the story is authentic and that Machiavelli's contemporaries knew of it, even though its meaning was contested even then. The original written record of it has disappeared, and what we know of the event follows the account of a Jesuit father, Stefano Binet (1569–1639). In his last moments, surrounded by his friends and relatives, Machiavelli described a dream he once had. He told how he first saw a crowd of poorly dressed men, and when he inquired about their identity, he was told that they were the blessed souls of Paradise. When they disappeared, another and larger group of individuals appeared. They had on courtly robes and bore themselves nobly. Upon closer examination, Machiavelli recognized Plato, Plutarch, and other noteworthy men of classical antiquity. When he inquired about this group, Machiavelli was told that they were souls condemned to eternal damnation. After they had also disappeared, Machiavelli was asked which group he preferred, and he instantly replied that he would rather be condemned to hell to discuss politics with such noble minds than to be in heaven with such a motley group.[11] This account has an unquestionable air of psychological veracity, for it provides a marvelous insight into Machiavelli's personality, his constant impulse to bring laughter into a life full of misfortune, and his view of life as an inseparable mixture of *cose grandi* and *cose vane*. After he told the story to his friends, he remained alone with his family, and, according to tradition, he received the last rites after confession.[12] Even as he faced death, Machiavelli never lost his sense of humor. A self-professed admirer of pagan culture until the last moment of his life and a severe critic of religion's practical effects upon worldly affairs, he nevertheless may have died within the church. If the story of his dream is true, it is further evidence that he viewed life in all of its intricacy. The letter in which he expressed his opinion about the imitation of nature is thus not only an important key to the style of Machiavelli's private correspondence; it also gives us an insight into Machiavelli's *forma mentis*. It is ironic that despite his constant interest in the art of portraiture in all of his works, Machiavelli's most enduring character sketch is that of himself. It was therefore fitting that the epitaph inscribed on Machiavelli's tomb, the tomb of a man who had eulogized and passed judgment on so many others, should read: "Tanto nomini nullum par elogium." [13]

Appendix
Machiavelli's Works

The following list contains the works discussed in this study (both Italian and English titles) as well as their dates of composition. The reader is reminded that many of these dates are still controversial.

1503:
Descrizione del modo tenuto dal duca Valentino nello ammazzare Vitellozzo Vitelli, Oliverotto da Fermo, il signor Pagolo e il duca di Gravini Orsini (*A Description of the Method Used by Duke Valentino in Killing Vitellozzo Vitelli, Oliverotto da Fermo, and Others*).

Parole da dirle sopra la provisione del danaio, fatto un poco di premio e di scusa (*Remarks on the Raising of Money*).

Del modo di trattare i popoli della Valdichiana ribellati (*On the Method of Dealing with the Rebellious Peoples of the Valdichiana*).

De natura gallorum (*On the French National Character*).

1508:
Rapporto delle cose della Magna (*Report on Germany*).

1509:
Discorso sopra le cose della Magna e sopra l'Imperatore (*Discourse on Germany and the Emperor*).

After 1512:
Ritratto delle cose della Magna (*Description of German Affairs*).

1512–1513:
Ritratto di cose di Francia (*Description of French Affairs*).

1513:
Il principe (*The Prince*).

1513–1519:
Discorsi sopra la prima deca di Tito Livio (*Discourses*).

After 1514:
Discorso o dialogo intorno alla nostra lingua (*A Dialogue on Language*).

1515–1520:
Belfagor.

1517–1518:
L'Asino d'oro (*The Golden Ass*).

1518:
Mandragola.

1519–1520:
L'arte della guerra (*The Art of War*).

1520:
La vita di Castruccio Castracani da Lucca (*The Life of Castruccio Castracani of Lucca*).

1520–1525:
Istorie fiorentine (*The History of Florence*).

1522:
Memoriale a Raffaello Girolami, quando ai 23 d'ottobre partí per Spagna all'imperatore (*Advice to Raffaello Girolami*).

1524–1525:
Clizia.

Last Years:
Esortazione alla penitenza (*An Exhortation to Penitence*).

Notes

Chapter 1

1. *History of Italian Literature*, trans. Joan Redfern (New York: Barnes and Noble, 1968), 2: 556.

2. *Machiavelli's Prince and its Forerunners: The Prince as a Typical Book De Regimine Principum* (Durham: Duke University Press, 1938).

3. For a discussion of Machiavelli's references to classical authors in his works, see Leslie J. Walker, ed., *The Discourses of Niccolò Machiavelli* (New Haven: Yale University Press, 1950), 2: 271–305.

4. Some of these studies, many largely speculative, are: A. H. Krappe, "Quelques sources grecques de Niccolò Machiavelli," *Études italiennes* 6 (1924): 80–86; William S. Anderson, "Livy and Machiavelli," *Classical Journal* 53 (1958): 232–35; Leo Strauss, "Machiavelli and Classical Literature," *RNL* 1 (1970): 7–25; Neal Wood, "Frontinus as a Possible Source for Machiavelli's Method," *JHI* 28 (1967): 243–48, and "Some Common Aspects of the Thought of Seneca and Machiavelli," *RenQ* 21 (1968): 11–23; and Gennaro Sasso, "La teoria dell'anacyclosis," pp. 161–222, and "Polibio e Machiavelli: costituzione, potenza, conquista," pp. 223–80, in *Studi su Machiavelli* (Naples: Morano, 1967).

5. "La istoria è la maestra delle azioni nostre, e massime de' principi, e il mondo fu sempre ad un modo abitato da uomini che hanno avuto sempre le medesimi passioni" (*ADG*, p. 73).

6. *Individuals in Thucydides* (Cambridge: Cambridge University Press, 1968), pp. 5–6.

7. Walker, 2: 286. Walker concludes that Machiavelli took relatively few quotations from Thucydides and that Thucydides's method had little effect upon the Florentine. He fails to mention the possibility of a stylistic influence, but the few times Machiavelli used this historian argues against this as well.

8. P. G. Walsh, *Livy: His Historical Aims and Methods* (Cambridge: Cambridge University Press, 1961), p. 109.

9. Ibid., pp. 82–88.

10. Anderson, p. 232.

11. *Livy with an English Translation*, trans. B. O. Foster (New York: G. P. Putnam's Sons, 1919), 1: 7.

12. Anderson, p. 235.

13. Walker, 2: 280.

14. R. H. Barrow, *Plutarch and His Times* (Bloomington: Indiana University Press, 1967), p. 162.

15. Walker, 2: 281–82.

16. "Habbiamo facto cercare delle Vite di Plutarco, et non se ne trouva in Firenze da vendere. Habbiate patientia, ché bisogna scrivere ad Venetia; et a dirvi il vero, voi siate lo 'nfracida ad chiedere tante cose" (L, p. 82). It should be noted that this edition of Machiavelli's letters contains letters he received as well as those he himself wrote.

17. "Il segretario fiorentino," in Scritti su Machiavelli (Turin: Einaudi, 1964), p. 259.

18. Plutarch, The Lives of the Noble Grecians and Romans, trans. John Dryden (New York: Random House, n.d.), p. 293.

19. Ibid., p. 801.

20. Quoted from De legibus (1.5) by Michael Grant in Roman Literature (London: Penguin, 1958), p. 82.

21. Ibid.

22. For an interesting history of the transition of the exemplum from the rhetoric schools to the novella, see Salvatore Battaglia, "L'esempio medievale," FeL 6 (1959): 45–82, and "Dall'esempio alla novella," FeL 7 (1960): 21–84. Guido A. Guarino's introduction to his translation of Boccaccio's Concerning Famous Women (New Brunswick: Rutgers University Press, 1963) traces the influence of the "exemplarism" of Boccaccio's Latin works upon the Decameron. For a detailed treatment of the influence of rhetoric upon medieval literature, see Ernst Robert Curtius, European Literature and the Latin Middle Ages, trans. Willard R. Trask (New York: Harper & Row, 1963).

23. See Franco Simone, "Note sulla fortuna del Petrarca in Francia nella prima metà del Cinquecento," GSLI 127 (1950): 1–59, for a study of the influence of Petrarch's Latin works in France before his Canzoniere became popular. Patricia A. Gathercole chronicles the many translations of Boccaccio's Latin works into French, beginning with a 1409 translation of De casibus, in "The French Translators of Boccaccio," Italica 46 (1969): 300–309.

24. Giovanni Boccaccio, The Fates of Illustrious Men, trans. Louis Brewster Hall (New York: Ungar, 1965), pp. 231–32.

25. For a discussion of the theory and practice of humanist historiography, see Felix Gilbert, Machiavelli and Guicciardini: Politics and History in Sixteenth-Century Florence (Princeton: Princeton University Press, 1965), esp. pp. 203–35, and a bibliographical essay, "Humanist Historiography," pp. 332–35. Also useful are Lauro Martines, The Social World of the Florentine Humanists: 1390–1460 (Princeton: Princeton University Press, 1963); Nancy S. Struever, The Language of History in the Renaissance: Rhetoric and Historical Consciousness in Florentine Humanism (Princeton: Princeton University Press, 1970); and Donald J. Wilcox, The Development of Florentine Humanist Historiography in the Fifteenth Century (Cambridge: Harvard University Press, 1969).

26. Felix Gilbert, p. 238. See also Felix Gilbert's Niccolò Machiavelli e la vita culturale del suo tempo, trans. Alda de Capariis (Bologna: Il

mulino, 1964), esp. the essay entitled "Introduzione alle *Istorie fiorentine*," pp. 230-40.

27. "Ho trovato come nella descrizione delle guerre fatte dai Fiorentini con i principi e popoli forestieri sono stati diligentissimi, ma delle civili discordie e delle intrinseche inimicizie, e degli effetti che da quelle sono nati, averne una parte al tutto taciuta e quell'altra in modo brevemente descritta che ai leggenti non puote arrecare utile o piacere alcuno" (*IF*, p. 68).

28. According to students of historiography, history ceased to be literature and became a science only in the late eighteenth century when historians first began to distinguish between original source materials and derivative authorities. For a discussion of this question, see Arnaldo Momigliano, "Ancient History and the Antiquarian," *JWCI* 13 (1950): 285-315, reprinted in *Studies in Historiography* (London: Weidenfeld & Nicolson, 1966), pp. 1-39; or George Huppert, *The Idea of Perfect History: Historical Erudition and Historical Philosophy in Renaissance France* (Urbana: University of Illinois Press, 1970), p. 5.

29. For a detailed analysis of this topic, see Curtius, pp. 167-82.

30. Expanding on Curtius's discussion, John H. Geerken, "Homer's Image of the Hero in Machiavelli: A Comparison of Areté and Virtù," *IQ* 14 (1970): 45, makes a distinction between literary heroes (celebrated for what they *are* or represent) and historical heroes (praised for what they *do* or achieve). Such a distinction is, to my mind, an arbitrary one and does not hold when applied to Machiavelli's major characters, who normally combine both admirable personal qualities and laudable deeds.

31. For the relationship of Machiavelli and Adriani, see ibid., pp. 47, 84. Adriani made a commentary on the first three books of the *Iliad*.

32. For a discussion of these medieval biographies and a refutation of Burckhardt's position, see Johan Huizinga, *The Waning of the Middle Ages: A Study of the Forms of Life, Thought and Art in France and the Netherlands in the Dawn of the Renaissance* (Garden City: Doubleday, 1954), pp. 67-77.

Chapter 2

1. *Nuovi studi sul linguaggio del Machiavelli* (Florence: Le Monnier, 1969), p. 168. Chiappelli's conclusions are the same in two other articles on the same topic: "I primi sviluppi del pensiero e del linguaggio del Machiavelli," *Approdo* 14 (1968): 65-86, and "Machiavelli as Secretary," *IQ* 14 (1970): 27-44.

2. For a discussion of the more than 6,000 autograph texts in the *Archivio di Stato* in Florence, documents covering the business of the Florentine Chancellery during the time Machiavelli was its Second Secretary, see Chiappelli, "Machiavelli as Secretary," ibid.; Gian Roberto Sarolli, "The Unpublished Machiavelli," *RNL* 1 (1970): 78-92, and "Un dichirografo inedito del Machiavelli 'dictante' e 'scribente,'" *MLN* 80 (1965): 41-62; and E. Dupré-Theseider, *Niccolò Machiavelli diplomatico* (Como: Marzorati, 1945).

Edouard-Felix Guyon, "Machiavel agent diplomatique," *Revue d'histoire diplomatique* 81 (1967): 97–124, and Nicolai Rubinstein, "The Beginnings of Niccolò Machiavelli's Career in the Florentine Chancery," *IS* 11 (1956): 72–91, both discuss Machiavelli's political responsibilities as Second Secretary. Federico Chabod, *Scritti su Machiavelli*, pp. 241–368, and J. R. Hale, *Machiavelli and Renaissance Italy* (New York: Collier, 1966), pp. 35–124, examine the literary affinities between Machiavelli's diplomatic correspondence and his later works, although neither deals in detail with the stylistic problem of Machiavelli's art of portraiture in his complete works.

 3. Chabod, p. 287.

 4. "Bisogna aspettare el tempo, che è padre della verità" (*LC* 2: 600).

 5. "Altro non ho che scrivere alle S. V. se non che se quelle mi domandessero quello che io creda di questi moti risponderei *praestita venia*" (*LC* 1: 370).

 6. "*Tamen* voi fate una conclusione troppo gagliarda quando voi scrivete" (*L*, p. 90).

 7. "Se alcuna cosa à detta temerariamente, è che noi vogliamo piuttosto scrivendo e errando, offendere noi, che non scrivendo e errando, mancare alla città" (*LC* 1: 136).

 8. "E, per venire ai particolari, dico che voi avete a osservare la natura dell'uomo, se si governa o lasciasi governare, se egli è avaro o liberale, se egli ama la guerra o la pace, se la gloria lo muove o altra sua passione" (*ADG*, p. 286).

 9. Between the time Machiavelli wrote this dispatch from France and the composition of *The Prince* (1513), he had changed his mind on the effects of miserliness. In *The Prince*, he prefers miserliness to profligacy, since miserliness may enable a man to retain control of his power while profligacy will most certainly cause him to lose the ability to defend himself: "Uno principe . . . debbe, s'elli è prudenta, non si curare del nome del misero" (*PD*, p. 67).

 10. "La natura sua respettiva allo spendere . . . di volerne trarre e non mettervi, e penser piú al comodo presente che ad quello gliene possessi resultare poi" (*LC* 1: 124).

 11. "Prudentissima, e li orecchi lunghi e il creder corto, e che la udiva ogni cosa, ma la prestava fede ad quello che la toccava con mano esser vero" (*LC* 1: 205).

 12. "E questo Re, né dormendo né vegghiando, sogna altro che il torto il pare ricevere da Sua Santità, né ha animo altro che la vendetta" (*LC* 3: 1320). Chabod, pp. 372–73, defines Machiavelli's typical presentation of a situation as a "procedere dilemmatico" or a "dilemma-like" procedure, a tendency to define political problems in terms of two extreme, antithetical solutions, ignoring any middle ground of compromise. J. H. Whitfield, *Machiavelli* (Oxford: Blackwell's, 1947), p. 44, calls this same stylistic trait the "classical Machiavellian *aut-aut*," referring to the particular "either/or" form that Machiavelli's "procedere dilemmatico" often takes, as in this sen-

tence from *The Prince*: "Sono, questi dominii cosí acquistati, o consueti a vivere sotto uno principe, o usi a essere liberi; et acquistonsi, o con le arme d'altri o con le proprie, o per fortuna o per virtú" (*PD*, p. 15, my italics). For a discussion of how such a technique hinders Machiavelli in logical, systematic explanations of his political ideas, see Sydney Anglo, *Machiavelli: A Dissection* (London: Victor Gollancz, 1969), pp. 238–69.

13. "Disarmati in mezo de' nimici" (*LC* 3: 1329).

14. "Di qui nacque che tutt'i profeti armati vinsono, e li disarmati ruinorono" (*PD*, p. 32).

15. "Perché el Re non essendo uso minutamente ad governare queste cose, le straccura; e questi che le governono ora non pigliono per loro medesimi autorità veruna, non che di fare, ma di ricordare che si faccia: e cosí mentre che el medico non vi pensa, e il servigiale lo straccura, el malato si muore. E, parlando io oggi con Rubertet, venne un dipintore che portò la immagine del Legato morto, in sulla quale dopo un sospiro disse: o padrone mio, se tu fussi vivo, noi saremmo con el nostro esercito ad Roma: le quali parole mi confermorono piú in quello che di sopra vi scrivo" (*LC* 3: 1334).

16. In chapter three, Machiavelli uses the famous metaphor of "medecine forti" for "drastic measures." In an even more notable example in the same chapter, Machiavelli says: "Perché e Romani feciono in questi casi quello che tutti e principi savvi debbono fare: li quali non solamente hanno ad avere riguardo alli scandoli presenti, ma a' futuri, et a quelli con ogni industria obviare, perché, prevendendosi discosto, facilmente vi si può rimediare, ma, aspettando che ti si appressini, la medecina non è a tempo, perché la malattia è diventata incurabile" (*PD*, p. 21). It is more than co-incidence that this particular chapter discusses both Louis XII and the cardinal. There must be some link between the imagery of this dispatch and this later chapter of *The Prince* which employs similar metaphors for state-craft. Chiappelli, "Machiavelli as Secretary," p. 34, has found examples of this same imagery from dispatches dating as early as 1498. For a general treatment of this question, see Paul Archambault, "The Analogy of the Body in Renaissance Political Literature," *BHR* 29 (1967): 21–53.

17. "Che l'Imperadore abbi assai soldati e buoni, nessuno ne dubita; ma come li possa tenere insieme, qui sta el dubbio: perché non li tendendo lui se non per forza di danari, e avendone da un canto scarsità per se stesso, quando non ne sia provveduto da altri (che non si può sapere), dall'altro sendone troppo liberale, si aggiunge difficultà ad difficultà; e benché essere liberale sia vertú nei principi, *tamen* e' non basta satisfare ad mille uomini, quando altri ha bisogno di ventimila" (*LC* 2: 1099).

18. "Ma è tanto buono e umano signore, che viene ad essere troppo facile e credulo; d'onde ne nasce, che qualcuno dubita di questa mossa nel modo soprascritto" (*LC* 2: 1099).

19. Chabod, pp. 280–81, is firmly convinced that "these letters from France . . . are almost all written in Machiavelli's hand."

20. *Machiavelli and the Renaissance*, p. 97.

21. Sergio Bertelli, *LC* 2: 1101. For a discussion of Machiavelli's

handwriting and the problems involved in dealing with the manuscripts in the Florentine archives, see Paolo Ghiglieri, *La grafia del Machiavelli studiata negli autografi* (Florence: Leo S. Olschki, 1969).

22. In *Machiavelli e Cesare Borgia: storia di un giudizio* (Rome: Ateneo, 1966), p. 41, Gennaro Sasso has serious doubts to the thesis that the first two letters from the mission were written by Machiavelli and simply signed by Soderini. He concludes that they are the work of both men, the harmonious product of their collaboration. Chiappelli, "Machiavelli as Secretary," p. 30, distinguishes three groups of Chancellery documents. There are those dispatches, like the letters from the second mission to Borgia at Imola or the first mission to Rome, written directly by Machiavelli when he was alone and fully responsible for determining the subject matter and style of the letters. Other dispatches were written by Machiavelli while he was a member of a mission committee, and thus he was forced to speak for a group. Finally, there are dispatches, like those from Urbino, written by Machiavelli in the name of his superior. These are often signed by the superior in spite of the fact that Machiavelli wrote them himself, or wrote them with at least the approval and collaboration of his superior Soderini.

23. "Sua Signoria, sanza molto circuito di parole, disse: . . . troppo ben conosco che la città vostra non ha buono animo verso di me; anzi mi lascerà come uno assasino; et hanno cerco darmi grandissimi carichi et con el Papa et con el re di Francia. Questa ultima parte si negò e confutò l'altra ricercámoci dichiarassi meglio. Disse: Io so ben siete prudente et m'intendete, pure ve lo ridirò in breve parole. Questo governo non mi piace et mi facciate cauto della osservanzia di quello mi promettessi: altrimenti voi intenderete presto presto che io non voglio vivere ad questo modo: et se non mi vorrete amico, mi proverete inimico" (*LC* 1: 262–63).

24. "Questo Signore è molto splendido et magnifico, et nelle armi è tanto animoso, che non è sí gran cosa che non li paia piccola, et per gloria et per acquistare stato mai si riposa né conosce fatica o periculo: giunge prima in un luogo, che se ne possa intendere la partita donde si lieva; ha cappati e' migliori uomini d'Italia: le quali cose lo fanno vittorioso et formidabile, aggiunto con una perpetua fortuna" (*LC* 1: 267–68).

25. *Machiavelli's The Prince: A Bilingual Edition*, ed. and trans. Mark Musa (New York: St. Martin's, 1964), p. xv. For other important studies of the meaning of this key term in Machiavelli's works, see Felix Gilbert, "On Machiavelli's Idea of Virtù," *Renaissance News* 4 (1951): 53–55, and 5 (1952): 21–33; J. H. Whitfield, "The Doctrine of Virtù," *IS* 3 (1946): 28–33; and Neal Wood, "Machiavelli's Concept of Virtù Reconsidered," *Political Studies* 15 (1967): 160–72.

26. Musa.

27. "The Perspective of Art," *KR* 15 (1953): 175–76.

28. "E chi esamina la qualità dell'una parte e dell'altra conosce questo Signore uomo animoso, fortunato e pieno di speranza; favorito da un Papa e da un Re, e da costoro iniurato, non *solum* in uno stato che voleva acquistare, ma in uno che egli aveva acquistato" (*LC* 1: 392).

29. In chapter seven of *The Prince*, Machiavelli gives a rather un-

convincing explanation of this singular execution—he claims that the severity of Remirro's rule was no longer necessary to control the province. In fact, Machiavelli failed to see the real significance of this murder. Borgia sacrificed his trusted lieutenant to beguile the conspirators of Magione into his trap at Sinigaglia.

30. "Venne Vitellozzo in su una muletta, disarmato, con una gabbanella in dosso stretta, nera e lorgora, e di sopra uno gabbano nero foderato di verde; e chi lo avessi veduto, non arebbe mai giudicato che fussi colui che due volte questo anno e' suoi auspicii avea cerco cacciare el re di Francia di Italia. Era el volto suo pallido e attonito, che denotava ad ciascuno facilmente la sua futura morte" (*LC* 1: 536).

31. Sasso, *Machiavelli e Cesare Borgia*, pp. 84–85.

32. "Vario, inresoluto e sospettoso, e non stare fermo in alcuna conclusione" (*LC* 2: 631).

33. "Il Duca gli pareva uscito del cervello, perché non sapeva lui stesso quello si volessi fare, sí era avviluppato e irresoluto" (*LC* 2: 632).

34. "Perché gli è noto el naturale odio che sua Santità li ha sempre portato, e non può sí presto avere smenticato lo esilio, nel quale è stato dieci anni; et el Duca si lascia trasportare da quella sua animosa confidenza; e crede che le parole d'altri sieno per essere piú ferme che non sono sute le sue" (*LC* 2: 599–600).

35. "E vedesi che questo Papa comincia ad pagare e' debiti suoi assai onorevolmente, e li cancella con la bambagia del calamaio; da tutti non di meno gli sono benedette le mani, e li fieno tanto piú, quanto si andrà piú avanti" (*LC* 2: 683).

36. "E poiché gli è preso, o vivo o morto che sia, si può fare sanza pensare piú al caso suo" (*LC* 2: 683).

37. "Vedesi che e' pecatti sua lo hanno a poco a poco condotto alla penitenza" (*LC* 2: 689).

38. Sasso, *Machiavelli e Cesare Borgia*, pp. 48, 77.

39. Sasso also ignores a fact emphasized in chapter one of this book, that Machiavelli requested a copy of Plutarch's *Vitae Parallelae* not during the Urbino mission but during his stay in Imola. If he had really been interested only in making a sketch of a "classicized" hero as Sasso maintains, it would have been more logical for him to have requested the copy of Plutarch during his stay in Urbino. While Sasso has Machiavelli turning from Borgia as a symbol "non letterario e retorico" to what he calls "un modello e un simbolo . . . politico," Machiavelli is in fact doing just the reverse: he is paying more attention to style in his own dispatches than in those written with Soderini at Urbino.

Chapter 3

1. "Queste due parti, la liberalità e la facilità, che lo fanno laudare a molti, sono quelle che lo ruinano" (*ADG*, p. 200).

2. "Ma son tanti gli uomini e tante le cose che gli può toccare d'esser ingannato ogni dí, quando e' se ne avvedesse sempre" (*ADG*, p. 202).

3. "Dirò solo di nuovo della natura dell'Imperatore, quale è uomo gittatore del suo sopra tutti gli altri che a' nostri tempi o prima sono stati; il che fa che sempre ha bisogno, né somma alcuna è per bastargli in qualunque grado o fortuna si trovi. È vario, perché oggi vuole una cosa e domani no; non si consiglia con persona, e crede ad ognuno: vuole le cose che non può avere, e da quelle che può avere si discosta, e per questo piglia sempre i partiti al contrario. . . . È umano quando da udienza, ma la vuole dare a sua posta, né vuole essere corteggiato dagli ambasciadori se non quando egli manda per loro; è segretissimo; sta sempre in continue agitazioni d'animo e di corpo, ma spesso disfà la sera quello conclude la mattina" (ADG, p. 207).

4. "Perché li populi in privato sieno ricchi, la ragione è questa: che vivono come poveri, non edificono, non vestono e non hanno masserizie in casa; e basta loro abundare di pane, di carne, e avere una stufa dove rifuggire il freddo. . . . E cosí si godono questa loro rozza vita e libertà" (ADG, pp. 209–210).

5. For a perceptive treatment of the significance of Machiavelli's use of the word *rozzo* ("rough") and its political implications, see Daniel Waley, "The Primitivist Element in Machiavelli's Thought," *JHI* 31 (1970), 91–98. A more general treatment of Tacitus and Machiavelli is G. Toffanin's *Machiavelli e il 'Tacitismo'* (Padua: A Draghi, 1921).

6. "Per natura sono piú fieri che gagliardi o destri" (ADG, p. 167); "La natura de' Franzesi è appetitosa di quello d'altri" (ADG, p. 170):

7. "Cesar disse e Franzesi essere in principio piú che uomini e in fine meno che femmine" (ADG, p. 168). The reference is in fact from Livy's *From the Founding of the City*. Machiavelli corrects himself in a reference to the French national character in the *Discourses* (bk. 3, ch. 36): "mi fa ricordare di quello che Tito Livio piú volte dice: che i Franciosi sono nel principio della zuffa piú che uomini, e nel successo del combattere riescono poi meno che femine. E pensando donde questo nasca, si crede per molti che sia la na tura loro cosí fatta: il che credo sia vero" (PD, p. 484).

8. "Dicendomi el cardinale di Roano che li Italiani non si intendevano della guerra, io li resposi ch'e' Franzesi non si intendevano dello stato" (PD, p. 25).

9. "Stimono tanto l'utile e il danno presente, che cade in loro poca memoria delle iniurïe o benifizii passati, e poca cura del bene o male futuro" (ADG, p. 157).

10. "Sono piú cupidi de' danari che del sangue" (ADG, p. 157); "Sono liberali solo nelle audienze" (ADG, p. 157).

11. "Sono nimici del parlare romano e della fama loro" (ADG, p. 158).

12. I refer to the first and last of these works by shortened English titles. The complete Italian titles are listed in the Appendix.

13. Although the editor of the minor works, Sergio Bertelli, rejects this theory (ADG, p. 52), other scholars view the work as an imaginary speech. Chabod, *Scritti su Machiavelli*, p. 324, admits that the work could

be a *"ghiribizzo,* written by Machiavelli, to clarify his other works"; Hale, *Machiavelli and the Renaissance,* p. 72, simply calls the work an "imaginary speech." The most convincing argument is that of Allan H. Gilbert in *Machiavelli: The Chief Works and Others* (Durham: Duke University Press, 1965), 3: 1439, who notes that on the autograph manuscript, Machiavelli has written "1503, March — Oration," using the same word for oration (*concione*) that he applies to his imaginary speeches in the dedication of *The History of Florence.* For an interesting treatment of the term *ghiribizzo* (fantasy) and another word Machiavelli uses with a similar meaning, *castelluccio* (project, often in the sense of an imaginary idea), see Franco Masciandaro's "I 'castellucci' e i 'ghiribizzi' del Machiavelli epistolografo," *Italica* 46 (1969): 135–48, or his unpublished master's thesis, "Machiavelli Epistolografo" (Tulane University, 1966).

14. "Queste due cose el nervo di tutte le signorie, che furno o che saranno mai al mondo" (*ADG,* p. 57).

15. "Come sentirno sonare le artiglierie nelle lor mura e fremer lo esercito de' nemici, corsono piangendo allo 'mperadore con grembi pieni di danari; e' quali lui cacciò via, dicendo: Andate a morire con cotesti danari, poi che voi non avete voluto vivere sanza essi" (*ADG,* p. 61).

16. "Ma non bisogna che io vadia in Grecia per li esempli, avendogli in Firenze" (*ADG,* p. 61).

17. Alessandro Montevecchi, "Le prime operette di Machiavelli: elementi dello stile storico," *Convivium* 33 (1965): 152–61, sees this work as the most important minor work of Machiavelli. This judgment cannot be substantiated, since *A Description of the Method Used by Duke Valentino in Killing Vitellozzo Vitelli, Oliverotto da Fermo, and Others* is more important stylistically (especially for Machiavelli's art of portraiture), and *On the Method of Dealing with the Rebellious Peoples of the Valdichiana* is a clearer theoretical explanation of Machiavelli's view of history as a didactic process.

18. Most critics agree with this assessment, although few analyze this work in detail as I do here. Hale, *Machiavelli and the Renaissance,* p. 71, simply calls the work a "literary version of the Senigallia episode"; Chabod, *Scritti su Machiavelli,* p. 317, believes the work is constructed in a literary manner. For an analysis of this work and its relation to Machiavelli's art of portraiture, see Peter E. Bondanella, "The Style and Function of Machiavelli's Character Sketches," *FI* 4 (1970): 58–69, which forms the basis of the present discussion.

19. "Parse loro come el duca diventassi troppo potente, e che fussi da temere che occupata Bologna e' non cercassi di spegnerli per rimanere solo in su l'armi in Italia" (*ADG,* p. 41).

20. "Non solo non si a derirno loro ma mandorno Niccolò Machiavegli loro secretario a offerire al duca ricetto e aiuto contro a questi suoi nuovi inimici. El quale si trovava pieno di paura in Imola, perché in un tratto e fuori d'ogni sua opinione, sendogli diventati inimici e' soldati sua, si trovava con una guerra propinqua e disarmato" (*ADG,* pp. 42–43).

21. In the instructions from his superiors in the Chancellery,

Machiavelli is ordered simply to declare Florence's friendship for Borgia in vague terms, but this affirmation of general friendship was all that the envoy was permitted to make: "E questo ci pare che debbi bastare per la tua prima audienzia . . . né vogliamo che fuori di questo in questa materia tu parli di altro o altrimente: e di ciò che sua Eccellenzia ti ricercassi piú oltre, rimetter'ti a darcene avviso, e aspettare risposta" (*LC* 1: 336). Borgia rightly interpreted this offer of "friendship" as a refusal of any positive assistance from Florence in Machiavelli's historically accurate account of the mission.

22. "Ripreso animo in su l'offerta de' Fiorentini, disegnò temporeggiare la guerra con quelle poche genti che aveva e con pratiche di accordi" (*ADG*, p. 43).

23. Renzo Sereno, "A Falsification by Machiavelli," *Renaissance News* 12 (1959): 159–67, reports on a manuscript in Machiavelli's own hand in the Central Library of Florence which is an elaboration by Machiavelli of a circular order of Borgia wherein Machiavelli has even imitated the Duke's signature. Sereno asserts that Machiavelli "derived deep if infantile pleasure from seeing his handwriting coupled with Caesar's signature" (p. 164), and that his imitation of Borgia's order was motivated by the fantasy of being near real power in a vicarious manner through copying the document, a position he never attained in his own political career.

24. "Ed essendo grandissimo simulatore, non mancò di alcuno oficio a fare intendere loro come eglino avieno mosso l'armi contro a colui che ciò che aveva acquistato voleva che fussi loro, e come gli bastava avere el titolo del principe ma che voleva che 'l principato fussi loro" (*ADG*, p. 43).

25. "Benché si trovassi già sí forte che potessi con guerra aperta vendicarsi contro a' suoi inimici, nondimanco pensò che fussi piú securo e piú utile modo ingannarli e non fermare per questo le pratiche dello accordo" (*ADG*, pp. 43–44).

26. "E Vitellozzo disarmato, con una cappa foderata di verde, tutto afflitto come se fussi conscio della sua futura morte, dava di sé (conosciuta la virtú dello uomo e la passata sua fortuna) qualche ammirazione. E si dice che quando e' si partí da le sua genti per venire a Sinigaglia e andare contro al duca, ch'e' fece come una ultima dipartenza con quelle: e a li suoi capi raccomandò la sua casa e le fortune di quella, ed e' nipoti ammuní che non della fortuna di casa loro, ma della virtú de' loro padri e de' loro zii si ricordassino" (*ADG*, p. 47).

27. *Machiavelli e Cesare Borgia*, p. 88. Since Sasso is only interested in Borgia as a subject of Machiavelli's political judgment, he ignores problems of style. It is mistaken to view the Imola dispatches as superior to this literary work except in so far as the description of Vitellozzo's arrival at Sinigaglia is a more highly wrought example of symbolic physical description in the letters.

28. "Chi ha osservato Cesare Borgia, detto il duca Valentino, vede che lui, quanto a mantenere gli stati ch'egli ha, non ha mai disegnato fare fondamento in su amicizie italiane, avendo sempre stimato poco i Viniziani, e voi meno: il che quando sia vera, conviene che e' pensi di farsi tanto stato in Italia che lo faccia sicuro per se medesimo e che faccia da un altro

potentato l'amicizia sua desiderabile. . . . resta ora vedere se gli è il tempo accomodato a colorire questi suoi disegni" (*ADG*, p. 75).

29. Sarolli, "The Unpublished Machiavelli," pp. 83–84, asserts that Machiavelli "actually created either a new word for the traditional vocabulary of the Chancery or a new genre which, unfortunately, was not absorbed into the Italian tradition but was destined to a better reception in French political literature. The new word is *ritratto*." The Italian titles for two of the works discussed in this chapter, *Description of German Affairs* and *Description of French Affairs*, contain this word *ritratto* (*Ritratto delle cose della Magna* and *Ritratto di cose di Francia*). Sarolli is correct in noting that this word is important in the vocabulary of Machiavelli's early letters and works, but he leaves the impression that it was Machiavelli who invented the genre of the "character sketch," a genre that became famous through La Bruyère in France. While Machiavelli does practice the art of character sketches in his works, they are normally set within a broader political framework and lack the aphoristic quality normally associated with this genre. Gilbert Highet, *The Classical Tradition: Greek and Roman Influences on Western Literature* (New York: Oxford University Press, 1967), p. 192, traces the development of the genre from Theophrastus and Isaac Casaubon (who edited Theophrastus's works in 1592) to La Bruyère, Hall, Earle, and Addison. The word *ritratto*, however, passed into the English language in the eighteenth century and was used to denote an artistic sketch. For a history of the word, see Carlo Battisti and Giovanni Alessio, *Dizionario etimologico italiano* (Florence: G. Babera, 1957), 5: 3267.

Chapter 4

1. "E' nuovi, o sono nuovi tutti, come fu Milano a Francesco Sforza, o sono come membri aggiunti allo stato ereditario del principe che li acquista, come è el regno di Napoli al re di Spagna" (*PD*, p. 15). For a good discussion of the kinds of exempla in *The Prince*, see Giorgio Bàrberi Squarotti, *La forma tragica del Principe e altri saggi sul Machiavelli* (Florence: Leo S. Olschki, 1966), pp. 145, 150–51.

2. "Noi abbiamo in Italia, *in exemplis*, el duca di Ferrara, il quale non ha retto alli assalti de' Viniziani nello '84, né a quelli di papa Julio nel '10, per altre cagioni che per essere antiquato in quello dominio" (*PD*, p. 16).

3. The traditional view that the *Discourses* were begun in 1513 and completed by 1519 (with an interruption during which Machiavelli wrote *The Prince*) has recently been challenged. For a detailed analysis of the arguments concerning the dating of the *Discourses*, see Erich W. Cochrane, "Machiavelli: 1940–1960," *Journal of Modern History* 33 (1961): 133–36.

4. "La cognizione delle azioni delli uomini grandi, imparata con una lunga esperienza delle cose moderne et una continua lezione delle antique" (*PD*, p. 13).

5. "Dimostrare a qualunque quanto le azioni degli uomini par-

ticulari facessono grande Roma e causassino in quella città molti buoni effetti" (*PD*, pp. 383–84).

6. "As when many archers aim at a target and none strikes it, the one who comes closest is without a doubt the best of all" (Dedication, pt. 3). I quote from *Baldassar Castiglione, Giovanni Della Casa: Opere*, ed. Giuseppe Prezzolini (Milan: Rizzoli, 1937), p. 51.

7. "Non si maravigli alcuno se, nel parlare che io farò de' principati al tutto nuovi e di principe e di stato, io addurrò grandissimi esempli; perché, camminando li uomini quasi sempre per le vie battute da altri, e procedendo nelle azioni loro con le imitazioni, né si potendo le vie d'altri al tutto tenere, né alla virtú di quelli che tu imiti aggiugnere, debbe uno uomo prudente intrare sempre per vie battute da uomini grandi, e quelli che sono stati eccellentissimi imitare, acciò che, se la sua virtú non vi arriva, almeno ne renda qualche odore: e fare come li arcieri prudenti, a' quali, parendo el loco dove disegnono ferire troppo lontano, e conoscendo fino a quanto va la virtú del loro arco, pongono la mira assai piú alta che il loco destinato, non per aggiugnere con la loro freccia a tanta altezza, ma per potere, con lo aiuto di sí alta mira pervenire al disegno loro" (*PD*, p. 30).

8. "Considerando adunque quanto onore si attribuisca all'antiquità, e come molte volte, lasciando andare infiniti altri esempli, un frammento d'una antiqua statua sia suto comperato gran prezzo, per averlo appresso di sé, onorarne la sua casa e poterlo fare imitare a coloro che di quella arte si dilettono, e come quegli dipoi con ogni industria si sforzono in tutte le loro opere rappresentarlo; e veggiendo da l'altro canto le virtuosissime operazioni che le istorie ci mostrono, che sono state operate da regni e da republiche antique, dai re, capitani, cittadini, latori di leggi ed altri che si sono per la loro patria affaticati, essere piú presto ammirate che imitate, anzi in tanto da ciascuno in ogni minima cosa fuggite, che di quella antiqua virtú non ci è rimasto alcun segno: non posso fare che insieme non me ne maravigli e dolga" (*PD*, pp. 123–24).

9. "Elli ha fatto el contrario di quelle cose che si debbono fare per tenere uno stato in una provincia disforme" (*PD*, p. 22).

10. "E fatto uno primo errore, fu costretto a seguitare; in tanto che, per porre fine alla ambizione di Alessandro, e perché non divenissi signore di Toscana, fu forzato venire in Italia. Non li bastò avere fatto grande la Chiesia e toltisi li amici, che, per volere el regno di Napoli, lo divise con il re di Spagna; e dove lui era, prima, arbitro d'Italia, e' vi misse uno compagno, acciò che li ambiziosi di quella provincia e mal contenti di lui avessino dove ricorrere" (*PD*, p. 23).

11. "Né è miraculo alcuno questo, ma molto ordinario e ragionevole" (*PD*, p. 25).

12. "Una regola generale, la quale mai o raro falla: che chi è cagione che uno diventi potente, ruina" (*PD*, p. 25).

13. "Io non saprei quali precetti mi dare migliori a uno principe nuovo, che lo esempio delle azioni sua" (*PD*, pp. 34–35).

14. "Si volse alli inganni; e seppe tanto dissimulare l'animo suo

che li Orsini, mediante el signor Paulo, si riconciliorono seco; con il quale el duca non mancò d'ogni ragione di offizio per assicurarlo, dandoli danari, veste e cavalli; tanto che la simplicità loro li condusse a Sinigallia nelle sua mani. Spenti adunque questi capi, e ridotti li partigiani loro amici sua, aveva il duca gittati assai buoni fondamenti alla potenza sua" (*PD*, p. 36).

15. "E, perché questa parte è degna di notizia, e da essere imitata da altri, non la voglio lasciare indrieto"; "Ma torniamo donde noi partimmo" (*PD*, p. 37).

16. Bàrberi Squarotti, pp. 157–58, discusses what he calls the "nonhistorical quality" of these exempla; Alessandro Montevecchi, "Lo stile delle *Storie fiorentine* di Machiavelli," *Sigma* 16 (1967): 84, agrees, saying that in *The Prince*, a chosen episode is taken out of its historical context for didactic purposes.

17. Geerken, "Homer's Image of the Hero in Machiavelli," p. 82.

18. "Bisogna adunque essere golpe a conoscere e' lasci, lione a sbigottire e' lupi" (*PD*, p. 72).

19. "Perché in Severo fu tanta virtú che, mantenendosi soldati amici, ancora che i populi fussino da lui gravati, possé sempre regnare felicemente; perché quelle sue virtú lo facevano nel conspetto de' soldati e de' populi sí mirabile, che questi rimanevano *quodammodo* attoniti e stupidi, e quelli altri reverenti e satisfatti. E perché le azioni di costui furono grandi in uno principe nuovo, io voglio monstrare brevemente quanto bene seppe usare la persona della golpe e del lione; le quali nature io dico di sopra essere necessarie imitare a uno principe" (*PD*, p. 80).

20. "Chi esaminerà adunque tritamente le azioni di costui, lo troverrà uno ferocissimo lione e una astutissima golpe . . . e non si maraviglierà se lui, uomo nuovo, arà possuto tenere tanto imperio" (*PD*, p. 81).

21. *Renaissance and Revolution: Backgrounds to Seventeenth-Century English Literature* (New York: Random House, 1967), p. 94; also found in his *Renaissance and Seventeenth-Century Studies* (New York: Columbia University Press, 1964), p. 157. This material originally appeared as an article, "Machiavelli: The Artist as Statesman," *UTQ* 31 (1962): 265–82.

22. Castiglione has one of his characters, Federigo Fregoso, suggest the topic of the book: "I would like our evening's game to be this: that one of our company be elected and be given the task of forming with words a perfect courtier" (bk. 1, pt. 12); translated from *Baldassar Castiglione, Giovanni Della Casa: Opere*, p. 68.

23. For this interpretation, see Luigi Russo, *Machiavelli* (Bari: Laterza, 1969), p. 85; and Salvatore Battaglia, *Mitografia del personaggio* (Milan: Rizzoli, 1968), p. 100.

24. "Tutto pietà, tutto fede, tutto integrità, tutto umanità, tutto relligione . . . li uomini in universali iudicano piú alli occhi che alle mani; perché tocca a vedere a ognuno, a sentire a pochi" (*PD*, p. 74).

25. Bàrberi Squarotti, pp. 232, 234.

26. *Machiavelli*, pp. 16–17. However, Bàrberi Squarotti, p. 241, finds a certain "tragic" and pessimistic quality in Machiavelli's protagonists.

27. Sayers discusses this aspect of Dante's characters in an introductory essay to her translation of *The Comedy of Dante Alighieri the Florentine: Hell* (Baltimore: Penguin, 1960), pp. 12–13.

28. In *The Theory of Literature* (New York: Harcourt, Brace and World, 1956), p. 189, René Wellek and Austin Warren see "recurrence and persistence" as the criteria for distinguishing between image and metaphor or symbol.

29. "Ma gli uomini pigliono certe vie del mezzo che sono dannosissime; perché non sanno essere né tutti cattivi né tutti buoni: come nel seguente capitolo per esemplo si mosterrà" (*PD*, p. 194).

30. "Nondimeno el Papa e il collegio sta ad discrezione di Giampaulo e non di loro: e se non farà male ad chi è venuto per torgli lo stato, sarà per sua buona natura e umanità . . . una volta Giampaulo dice avere conosciuto dua vie ad salvare lo stato suo; l'una con la forza, l'altra con la umiltà, e con el fidarsi delli amici che lo consigliano: e non ha voluto pigliare la prima, ma volgersi alla seconda" (*LC* 2: 980).

31. "Sí che portato da quel furore con il quale governava tutte le cose, con la semplice sua guardia si rimisse nelle mani del nimico; il quale dipoi ne menò seco lasciando un governatore in quella città che rendesse ragione per la Chiesa" (*PD*, p. 195).

32. "Fu notata, dagli uomini prudenti che col papa erano, la temerità del papa e la viltà di Giovampagolo; né potevono estimare donde si venisse che quello non avesse con sua perpetua fama oppresso ad un tratto il nemico suo, e sé arricchito di preda, sendo col papa tutti li cardinali con tutte le loro delizie" (*PD*, p. 195).

33. "Gli uomini non sanno essere onorevolmente cattivi o perfettamente buoni, e come una malizia ha in sé grandezza o è in alcuna parte generosa, e' non vi sanno entrare" (*PD*, p. 195).

34. "Cosí Giovampagolo, il quale non stimava essere incesto e publico parricida, non seppe, o a dir meglio non ardí, avendone giusta occasione, fare una impresa dove ciascuno avesse ammirato l'animo suo, e avesse di sé lasciato memoria eterna sendo il primo che avesse dimostro a' prelati quanto sia da stimare poco chi vive e regna come loro, ed avessi fatto una cosa la cui grandezza avesse superato ogni infamia, ogni pericolo che da quella potesse dependere" (*PD*, pp. 195–96).

35. Mazzeo, p. 122; also in his *Renaissance and Seventeenth-Century Studies*, p. 161.

36. Although Machiavelli is constantly identified with the phrase "the end justifies the means," he actually said in *The Prince* (ch. 18) that ends should be considered ("Si guarda al fine"), but he never bluntly said that any means is justified by a good end. Another statement in the same work, one usually ignored, is much closer to his true belief on this matter: "Yet it cannot be called *virtù* to kill one's fellow citizens, to betray friends, to be faithless, to be without mercy, to be without religion; all these qualities may enable one to acquire power but not glory." (*PD*, p. 42). Clearly in this passage, Machiavelli does not separate morality from political behavior.

37. Georges May explains the implications of the term for

Corneille's theatre in his introduction to *Pierre Corneille: Polyeucte and Le Menteur* (New York: Dell, 1963), p. 20.

38. Geerken, pp. 57–60, has an excellent discussion of the importance of conspiracies in Machiavelli's works.

39. "La quale come fu dentro, dalle mura rimproverò loro la morte del marito e minacciògli d'ogni qualità di vendetta. E per mostrare che de' suoi figliuoli non si curava, mostrò loro le membra genitali, dicendo che aveva ancora il modo a rifarne. Cosí costoro, scarsi di consiglio e tardi avvedutisi del loro errore, con una perpetua esilio patirono pene della poca prudenza loro" (*PD*, p. 408).

40. "Perché egli s'era fatto in modo popolare con le dimostrazioni, che pareva maraviglia ch'egli avesse preso sí presto una nuova natura e uno nuovo ingegno, essendo stato tenuto innanzi a questo tempo uno crudele perseguitatore della plebe" (*PD*, pp. 224–25).

41. "Ognuno vede quello che tu pari, pochi sentono quello che tu se'" (*PD*, p. 74).

42. "'Ille vero impedimentum pro occasione arripuit,' e nominò sé intra i primi, con maraviglia e dispiacere di tutti i nobili: nominò dipoi nove altri a suo proposito" (*PD*, pp. 225–26).

43. "Perché subito 'Appius finem fecit ferendae alienae personae'; e cominciò a mostrare la innata sua superbia, ed in pochi dí riempié de' suoi costumi i suoi compagni. E per isbigottire il popolo ed il Senato, in cambio di dodici littori ne feciono cento venti" (*PD*, p. 226).

44. "Donde nacque che s'innamorò di Virginia, e che volendola tòrre per forza, il padre Virginio per liberarla l'ammazzò; donde seguirono i tumulti di Roma e degli eserciti: i quali riduttisi insieme con il rimanente della plebe romana, se ne andarono nel Monte Sacro, dove stettero tanto che i Dieci deposero il magistrato e che furono creati i Tribuni ed i Consoli, e ridotta Roma nella forma della sua antica libertà" (*PD*, p. 227).

45. *Livy with an English Translation*, 2: 159.

46. Ibid., 2: 161.

47. "Oltre agli altri termini male usati da Appio per mantenere la tirannide, non fu di poco momento saltare troppo presto da una qualità a un'altra" (*PD*, pp. 229–30).

48. "Mutare in uno subito natura, e di amico mostrarsi inimico alla plebe, di umano superbo, di facile difficile, e farlo tanto presto che sanza scusa niuna ogni uomo avesse a conoscere la fallicia dello animo suo" (*PD*, p. 230).

49. *Dante: Poet of the Secular World*, trans. Ralph Manheim (Chicago: University of Chicago Press, 1961), pp. 177–78.

50. *Renaissance and Revolution*, p. 71; also found in his *Renaissance and Seventeenth-Century Studies*, p. 90.

Chapter 5

1. See, for example, Alfred O. Aldridge, "International Influences upon Biography as a Literary Genre," in *Actes du IVᵉ Congrès de l'Associa-*

tion Internationale de Littérature Comparée, ed. François Jost (The Hague: Mouton, 1966), 2: 975, who calls the work simply an "idealized portrait"; Guido A. Guarino, "Two Views of a Renaissance Tyrant," *Symposium* 10 (1956): 285, who describes the biography as "the best and most interesting fictionalized biography of the Renaissance"; Sidney Anglo, *Machiavelli: A Dissection*, p. 159; or Alessandro Montevecchi, "La vita di Castruccio Castracani e lo stile storico di Machiavelli," *Letterature Moderne* 12 (1962): 513–21, who concurs with this line of interpretation. None of these critics recognize the archetypal pattern of an heroic life in this biography though all admit that there is an element of idealization in the work. This chapter is an expanded version of an earlier essay, "Castruccio Castracani: Machiavelli's Archetypal Prince," *Italica* 49 (1972): 302–14.

2. "Machiavelli and Castruccio," *IS* 8 (1953), reprinted in J. H. Whitfield, *Discourses on Machiavelli*, p. 134.

3. Ibid., p. 124.

4. Ibid.

5. Robert Scholes and Robert Kellogg, *The Nature of Narrative* (Oxford: Oxford University Press, 1966), p. 66.

6. Peter Burke, *The Renaissance Sense of the Past* (New York: St. Martin's, 1970), p. 106; for a concurring view, see Felix Gilbert, "The Renaissance Interest in History," in *Art, Science, and History in the Renaissance*, ed. Charles S. Singleton (Baltimore: Johns Hopkins University Press, 1967), pp. 377–78.

7. *The Story of Art*, 11th ed., rev. (London: Phaidon, 1966), p. 141. It is interesting to note that Machiavelli's portrait of Castruccio is the literary counterpart of a popular artistic theme of the period, although most of the paintings and busts of Castruccio are now lost. For a treatment of this theme in Renaissance art, see Placido Campetti, "Ritratti di Castruccio Castracani," in *Castruccio Castracani degli Antelminelli: miscellanea di studi storici e letterari* (Florence, Tipocalcografia Classica, 1934), pp. 33–45.

8. *The Waning of the Middle Ages*, pp. 72, 74.

9. Ibid., pp. 74–75.

10. Alice M. Colby, *The Portrait in Twelfth-Century French Literature: An Example of the Stylistic Originality of Chrétien de Troyes* (Geneva: Droz, 1965), pp. 178–81.

11. "Hierarchical Patterns in the *Cantar de Mio Cid*," *RR* 53 (1962): 161–73.

12. *Heroic Song and Heroic Legend*, trans. B. J. Timmer (London: Oxford University Press, 1963), p. 210. For my discussion of the stages in this heroic pattern (based primarily upon classical and medieval literary texts), I am indebted to De Vries, especially pp. 210–26.

13. Ibid., p. 216.

14. For a lucid application of Wittgenstein's term "family resemblances" to generic classification, see E. D. Hirsch's *Validity of Interpretation* (New Haven: Yale University Press, 1967), especially the chapter entitled "The Concept of Genre," pp. 68–126.

15. "E' pare, Zanobi e Luigi carissimi, a quegli che la considerano,

cosa maravigliosa che tutti coloro o la maggiore parte di essi che hanno in questo mondo operato grandissime cose, e intra gli altri della loro età siano stati eccellenti, abbino avuto il principio e il nascimento loro basso e oscuro, o vero dalla fortuna fuora d' ogni modo travagliato; perché tutti o ei sono stati esposti alle fiere, o egli hanno avuto sí vil padre che, vergognatisi di quello, si sono fatti figliuoli di Giove o di qualche altro Dio. Quali sieno stati questi, sendone a ciascheduno noti molti, sarebbe cosa a replicare fastidiosa e poca acceta a chi leggessi; perciò come superflua la ometteremo" (*IF*, p. 9).

16. Geerken, "Homer's Image of the Hero in Machiavelli," p. 47. Adriani was one of the earliest Florentine commentators on Homer's works, having worked on the first three books of the *Iliad.*

17. "Fu adunque Castruccio Castracani da Lucca uno di quegli . . . e, come gli altri, non ebbe piú felice né piú noto nascimento, come nel ragionare del corso della sua vita si intenderà" (*IF*, p. 9).

18. "Occorse che andando una mattina, poco poi levata di sole, madonna Dianora (che cosí si chiamava la sirocchia di messer Antonio) a spasso per la vigna cogliendo secondo el costume delle donne certe erbe per farne certi suoi condimenti, sentí frascheggiare sotto una vite intra e' pampani, e rivolti verso quella parte gli occhi, sentí come piangere. Onde che tiratasi verso quello romore, scoperse le mani e il viso d'uno bambino che rinvolto nelle foglie pareva che aiuto le domandasse. . . . Presa adunque in casa una nutrice, con quello amore che se loro figliuolo fusse, lo nutrirono; e avendolo fatto battezzare, per il nome di Castruccio loro padre lo nominorono" (*IF*, pp. 10–11).

19. *The Hero with a Thousand Faces* (New York: Meridian, 1949), p. 319. In contrast to De Vries, who bases his study of the hero upon literary texts alone, Campbell uses additional information from legend, mythology, and Jungian psychology.

20. "Lasciati e' libri ecclesiastici da parte, cominciò a trattare le armi; né di altro si dilettava che o di maneggiare quelle, o con gli altri suoi equali correre, saltare, fare alle braccia e simili esercizii; dove ei mostrava virtú di animo e di corpo grandissima, e di lunga tutti gli altri della sua età superava. E se pure ei leggeva alcuna volta, altre lezioni non gli piacevano che quelle che di guerre o di cose fatte da grandissimi uomini ragionassino" (*IF*, p. 11).

21. "È cosa straordinaria a pensare in quanto brevissimo tempo ei diventò pieno di tutte quelle virtú e costumi che in uno vero gentile uomo si richieggono. In prima ei si fece uno eccellente cavalcatore, per che ogni ferocissimo cavallo con somma destrezza maneggiava; e nelle giostre e ne' torniamenti, ancora che giovinetto, era piú che alcuno altro riguardevole; tanto che in ogni azione o forte o destra non trovava uomo che lo superasse" (*IF*, p. 12).

22. "Ma sendo Uguccione aggravato nel male, si ritirò per curarsi a Montecarlo e lasciò a Castruccio la cura dello esercito" (*IF*, p. 15).

23. This battle plan is taken from Livy (23. 26–29) and is also discussed in Machiavelli's *The Art of War* (bk. 4).

24. "Ma Castruccio, di prigioniero diventato come principe di

Lucca, operò con gli amici suoi e con el favore fresco del popolo in modo che fu fatto capitano delle loro gente per un anno" (*IF*, p. 18).

25. "Venuti adunque sotto la fede di Stefano e di Castruccio, furono insieme con Stefano imprigionati e morti" (*IF*, p. 21).

26. Gaeta, *IF*, p. 22, n. 87, notes the invention of these victims. Whitfield, *Discourses on Machiavelli*, p. 125, believes that the entire episode of the capture of Pistoia is a modified version of an event in Xenophon's *Cyropaedia*, taken from a manuscript of Jacopo Poggio's Italian translation, finally printed in 1521.

27. Theodor E. Mommsen, "Castruccio Castracani and the Empire," in *Medieval and Renaissance Studies*, ed. Eugene F. Rice, Jr. (Ithaca: Cornell University Press, 1959), p. 19, notes that Castruccio used all these imperial titles in a will dated 20 December 1327.

28. Campbell, p. 356.

29. "Ma la fortuna, inimica alla sua gloria, quando era tempo di dargli vita gliene tolse, e interruppe quelli disegni che quello molto tempo innanzi aveva pensati di mandare ad effetto, né gliene poteva altro che la morte impedire. Erasi Castruccio nella battaglia tutto el giorno affaticato, quando, venuto el fine di essa, tutto pieno di affanno e di sudore, si fermò sopra la porta di Fucecchio per aspettare le genti che tornassino dalla vittoria e quelle con la presenzia sua ricevere e ringraziare . . . giudicando lo officio d'uno buono capitano essere montare il primo a cavallo e l'ultimo scenderne. Donde che, stando esposto a un vento che il piú delle volte a mezzo dí si leva di in su Arno, e suole essere quasi sempre pestifero, agghiacciò tutto: la quale cosa non essendo stimata da lui, come quello che a simili disagi era assuefatto, fu cagione della sua morte" (*IF*, pp. 32–33).

30. Gaeta, *IF*, p. 32, n. 132.

31. "Se io avessi creduto, figliuolo mio, che la fortuna mi avesse voluto troncare nel mezzo del corso il cammino per andare a quella gloria che io mi avevo con tanti miei felici successi promessa, io mi sarei affaticato meno e a te arei lasciato, se minore stato, meno inimici e meno invidia. . . . Ma la fortuna, che vuole essere arbitra di tutte le cose umane, non mi ha dato tanto giudicio che io l'abbi potuta prima conoscere, né tanto tempo che io l'abbi potuta superare" (*IF*, p. 33).

32. The classic argument for Machiavelli's absolute rejection of the *via di mezzo*, the target of Whitfield's argument, is Federico Chabod's "Metodo e stile di Machiavelli," in *Scritti su Machiavelli*, reprinted in Federico Chabod, *Machiavelli and the Renaissance*, trans. David Moore (New York: Harper & Row, 1958), pp. 126–48. Whitfield expands his thesis that the later works of Machiavelli argue the merits of compromise in "Machiavelli e la via di mezzo," *Problemi della Pedagogia* 4 (1958), reprinted in *Discourses on Machiavelli*, pp. 37–56. Raymond Crawford, *"Per quale iddio": Machiavelli's Second Thoughts* (Sidney: Sidney University Press, 1967), deals with Machiavelli's modifications of earlier opinions in his later works, including the reconsideration of moderation in political behavior.

33. Campbell, p. 30.

34. "Fu adunque Castruccio, per quanto si è dimostro, uno uomo

non solamente rare ne' tempi sua, ma in molti di quegli che innanzi erono passati. Fu della persona piú che l'ordinario di altezza, e ogni membro era all'altro rispondente; ed era di tanta grazia nello aspetto e con tanta umanità raccoglieva gli uomini, che non mai gli parlò alcuno che si partisse da quello mal contento. I capegli suoi pendevano in rosso, e portavagli tonduti sopra gli orecchi; e sempre, e d'ogni tempo, come che piovesse o nevicasse, andava con il capo scoperto" (IF, p. 35).

35. *Machiavelli and the Renaissance*, pp. 177–78.

36. Joseph Jay Deiss's *Captains of Fortune: Profiles of Six Italian Condottieri* (New York: Crowell, 1967), includes a portrait of Castruccio by an unknown contemporary artist. Deiss's book is a popular résumé of various sources (rarely acknowledged) of little scholarly merit. He even accepts many of the blatantly fabricated events in Machiavelli's biography as historical fact.

37. "Era ancora mirabile nel rispondere e mordere, o acutamente o urbanamente" (IF, p. 36).

38. In "I detti memorabili attribuiti a Castruccio Castracani da N. Machiavelli," *Castruccio Castracani degli Antelminelli*, pp. 217–60, Paolo Luiso first identified Diogenes Laertius as the source of most of these witty remarks. This work (printed as early as 1475 in Venice and Rome) was available to Machiavelli in a Latin translation. Machiavelli probably originally read about Castruccio in Niccolò Tegrimi's Latin biography, *Vita Castrucci Antelminelli Castracani Lucencis Ducis* (published in Modena in 1495) or in several medieval chronicles he might have known—a manuscript version of Villani's *Cronica* (especially book 10) or the anonymous *Storie Pistoresi*. Though Villani's history of Florence was not printed until after Machiavelli's death, Mirella Fonda-Bonardi's Ph.D. dissertation, "The *Istorie Fiorentine* by Niccolò Machiavelli" (University of California at Los Angeles, 1967), pp. 79–81, demonstrates that Machiavelli knew Villani's work well.

39. In *Wit and Wisdom of the Italian Renaissance* (Berkeley: University of California Press, 1964), pp. 1–15, Charles Speroni discusses the vogue of the *facetia* or witty anecdote and the general problem of wit in the Italian and European Renaissance. Poggio Bracciolini's *Facetiarum liber* began what became a separate literary genre, continued by Castiglione, Guazzo, Pontano, da Vinci, and many others.

40. "Visse quarantaquattro anni, e fu in ogni fortuna principe. . . . E perché vivendo ei non fu inferiore né a Filippo di Macedonia padre di Alessandro né a Scipione di Roma, ei morí nella età dell'uno e dell'altro; e senza dubbio avrebbe superato l'uno e l'altro se, in cambio di Lucca, egli avessi avuto per sua patria Macedonia o Roma" (IF, pp. 40–41).

41. "Quella vivacità . . . quella grandeza che si richiederebbe a un tanto huomo" (L, p. 394).

42. *Machiavelli and the Renaissance*, pp. 28–29.

Chapter 6

1. Felix Gilbert discusses the characteristics of humanist historiography — invented speeches, general reflections on a topic at the beginning of

each book, division of the narrative into sections, the use of history to teach by example — in *Niccolò Machiavelli e la vita culturale del suo tempo*, pp. 230–42. In my opinion, Gilbert overemphasizes the traditional aspect of Machiavelli's history. For example, he asserts that the invented speeches in humanist history were usually paired to present two sides of any important question. I have not found this so-called "traditional" form in *The History of Florence*, although Gilbert assumes that Machiavelli repeats all of the techniques found in the works of the humanists.

  2. "Se niuna cosa diletta o insegna nella istoria, è quella che particularmente si descrive" (*IF*, p. 69).

  3. Hale, *Machiavelli and Renaissance Italy*, p. 186, says that despite the admirable aspects of the work, "yet the general effect was lopsided and uneven . . . the effect is of an eccentric mask of events shaped over a concealed historical commentary"; Felix Gilbert, *Machiavelli and Guicciardini*, pp. 239, 292–93, 300–301, and *passim.*, consistently implies that Guicciardini's historical style and method are superior to Machiavelli's.

  4. *Machiavelli and Guicciardini*, p. 238.

  5. The *Cronica* of Giovanni Villani (c. 1270–1348) and the *Cronica di Dino Compagni delle cose accorrenti ne' tempi suoi* by Dino Compagni (c. 1255–1324) are both eyewitness accounts of the historical events of their day and are invaluable sources of information for the study of Florentine life in the medieval period. Machiavelli apparently obtained much of his raw material for his own work from, among others, Villani's *Cronica*. For an example of how far Machiavelli's style and view of history are separated from that of Villani, compare Villani's account of Castruccio Castracani (bks. 9–10) or of the Duke of Athens (bk. 12) to Machiavelli's biography of Castruccio or to his sketch of the Duke in *The History of Florence* which will be examined.

  6. "E se nel descrivere le cose seguite in questo guasto mondo non si narrerà o fortezza di soldati o virtú di capitano o amore verso la patria di cittadino, si vedrà con quali inganni, con quali astuzie e arti i principi, i soldati, i capi delle republiche, per mantenersi quella reputazione che non avevono meritata, si governavano. Il che sarà forse non meno utile che si sieno le antiche cose a cognoscere, perché, se quelle i liberali animi a seguitarle accendono, queste a fuggirle e spegnerle gli accenderanno" (*IF*, p. 327).

  7. *Machiavelli and Guicciardini*, p. 239.

  8. Ibid., pp. 168–69. Gilbert's assertion seems motivated by his desire to prove Guicciardini a more "modern" historian than Machiavelli. Guicciardini is more modern in his historical method, but it is not because Machiavelli is an allegorical writer.

  9. Charles S. Singleton examines this same type of presentation in the *Commedia* of Dante in "Dante's Allegory," in *American Critical Essays on the Divine Comedy*, ed. Robert J. Clements (New York: New York University Press, 1967), pp. 91–103. He argues that Dante's allegory is the "allegory of the theologians," not the "allegory of the poets." Rather than using characters

to mean something beyond themselves without having literal significance ("this *for* that"), Dante's symbolic characters combine both an historical, literal meaning with a symbolic meaning ("this *and* that").

10. Although Felix Gilbert, *Machiavelli and Guicciardini,* p. 238, views such episodes (bk. 4, ch. 6; bk. 5, ch. 32; bk. 7, ch. 20) where only one or two men are killed (usually by ridiculous accidents, such as falling off their horses) as satire of the humanist methods of writing history, the explanation may be much simpler. These three incidents comically illustrate how useless mercenary troops were as an instrument of Florentine foreign policy, since the mercenaries were more interested in pay and plunder than they were in carrying out Florence's political goals. Machiavelli's opinion of mercenary troops is treated at length in his *Arte della guerra.* For a detailed analysis of this work, see especially Neal Wood's introduction to his English edition, *The Art of War* (New York: Bobbs Merrill, 1965), pp. ix-lxxxvii; see also Giorgio Bàrberi Squarotti, "*L'arte della guerra* o l'azione impossibile," *LI* 20 (1968): 281–306; and Felix Gilbert, "Machiavelli: The Renaissance of the Art of War," in *The Makers of Modern Strategy,* ed. E. M. Earle (Princeton: Princeton University Press, 1944), pp. 3–25.

11. "Togliete per voi quelli beni che mi ha dati la fortuna e che voi mi potete tòrre; quelli che io ho dello animo, dove la gloria e l'onore mio consiste, né io vi darò né voi mi torrete!" (*IF,* p. 286).

12. "Esemplo veramente degno di quella lodata antichità! e tanto è piú mirabile di quelli, quanto è piú rado" (*IF,* p. 286).

13. "Non potette Agnolo sopportare la viltà e il malvagio animo di costui, e lo dette in preda a' suoi servidori, i quali dopo molti scherni gli davano solamente mangiare carte dipinte a biscie, dicendo che di guelfo per quel modo lo volemano fare diventare ghibellino: e cosí stentando, in brievi giorni morí" (*IF,* p. 286).

14. "Lo stile delle *Istorie fiorentine,*" p. 70.

15. "Voi vedete: questo palagio è vostro, e questa città è nelle vostre mani. Che vi pare che si faccia ora?" (*IF,* p. 245).

16. "Uomo sagace e prudente e piú alla natura che alla fortuna obligato" (*IF,* p. 245).

17. "E merita di essere annoverato intra i pochi che abbino beneficata la patria loro" (*IF,* p. 248).

18. Both Felix Gilbert (*Niccolò Machiavelli e la vita culturale del suo tempo,* p. 238), and Montevecchi ("Lo stile delle *Istorie fiorentine,*" p. 80), feel that this device is a traditional one, taken from the practice of the Latin humanists. However, Guicciardini uses a similar technique in chapters 1 and 9 of his *Storie fiorentine* in referring to Cosimo and Lorenzo de' Medici, in a work Gilbert claims "did not follow the humanist rules for historical writing" as his later two histories did (*Machiavelli and Guicciardini,* p. 230). Neither Gilbert nor Montevecchi cite similar examples of the *elogium* technique in either classical or humanist works.

19. "Aveva costui, per darsi reputazione, sempre opinione contraria ai piú potenti tenuta; e dove ei vedeva inclinare il popolo, quivi per farselo piú

benivolo la sua autorità voltava; in modo che di tutti i dispareri e novità era capo, e a lui rifuggivono tutti quelli che alcuna cosa estraordinaria di ottenere desideravono" (IF, p. 171).

20. "Questo fine ebbe messer Corso . . . e se gli avessi avuto lo animo piú quieto, sarebbe piú felice la memoria sua; nondimeno merita di essere numerato intra i rari cittadini che abbia avuti la nostra città" (IF, p. 173).

21. "Dello stato, se voi volete vivere sicuri, toglietene quanto ve ne è dalle leggi e dagli uomini dato: il che non vi recherà mai né invidia né pericolo, perché quello che l'uomo si toglie, non quello che all'uomo è dato, ci fa odiare; . . . Con queste arti io ho intra tanti nimici, intra tanti dispareri, non solamente mantenuta, ma accresciuta la reputazione mia in questa città. Cosí quando seguitiate le pedate mie manterrete e accrescerete voi" (IF, p. 292).

22. "Fu Giovanni misericordioso, e non solamente dava elemosine a chi le domandava, ma molte volte al bisogno de' poveri sanza essere domandato soccorreva. Amava ognuno, i buoni lodava e de' cattivi aveva compassione. Non domandò mai onori ed ebbegli tutti. Non andò mai in Palagio se non chiamato. Amava la pace, fuggiva la guerra. Alle aversità degli uomini suvveniva, le prosperità aiutava. Era alieno dalle rapine publiche e del bene comune aumentatore. Ne' magistrati grazioso; non di molta eloquenza, ma di prudenza grandissima. Mostrava nella presenza melanconico, ma era poi nella conversazione piacevole e faceto. Morí ricchissimo di tesoro ma piú di buona fama e di benivolenza. La cui eredità, cosí de' beni della fortuna come di quelli dell'animo, fu da Cosimo non solamente mantenuta ma accresciuta" (IF, pp. 292–93).

23. Montevecchi, "Lo stile delle Istorie fiorentine," p. 78, sees the whole passage as built upon the device of the chiasmus. This is not completely accurate if the definition of the term is taken precisely.

24. "E, perché dalla V. S. Beatitudine mi fu imposto particularmente e commandato che io scrivessi in modo le cose fatte da' Suoi maggiori, che si vedessi che io fussi da ogni adulazione discosto (perché quanto vi piace di udire degli uomini le vere lodi, tanto le finte e a grazia descritte le dispiacciano), dubito assai, nel descrivere la bontà di Giovanni, la sapienza di Cosimo, la umanità di Piero e la magnificenzia e prudenzia di Lorenzo, che non paia alla V. S. che abbia trapassati i comandamenti Suoi. E se sotto a quelle loro egregie opere era nascosta una ambizione alla utilità commune, come alcuni dicono, contraria, io che non ve la conosco non sono tenuto a scriverla; perché in tutte le mie narrazioni io non ho mai voluto una disonesta opera con una onesta cagione ricoprire, né una lodevole opera, come fatta a uno contrario fine, oscurare" (IF, pp. 65–66).

25. "Vero è che quando pure avviene (che avviene rade volte) che per buona fortuna della città surga in quella un savio, buono e potente cittadino da il quale si ordinino leggi per le quali questi umori de' nobili e de' popolani si quietino o in modo si ristringhino che male operare non possino, allora è che quella città si può stabile e fermo giudicare" (IF, p. 271).

26. In "The Humanist Portrait of Cosimo de' Medici, Pater Patriae," *JWCI* 24 (1961): 186–221, Alison M. Brown presents an excellent analysis of the many eulogies of Cosimo written during his lifetime which were collected after his death for presentation to Lorenzo. This *Collectiones Cosimanae*, now in the Biblioteca Laurenziana, contains prefaces of translations dedicated to Cosimo, orations, letters of consolation during his exile, and poetic elegies or epigrams. Brown notes that Cosimo was described in three different ways by three different groups of people. The early republican humanists (Bruni, Bracciolini) saw him as the prototype of the Roman lawgiver and statesman. Scholars such as Johannes Argyropoulos who were influenced by Aristotle's works saw him as the perfect ruler-philosopher. Men such as Ficino and Cristoforo Landino, who benefitted from Cosimo's patronage, praised him as a Maecenus or as an imperial Augustus. Brown only refers to Machiavelli's subsequent portrait of Cosimo in passing, but she sees Machiavelli's references to Cosimo's liberality, magnificence, prudence, and modesty as conforming quite closely to the classical panegyric. Machiavelli's interpretation of Cosimo seems closest to the republican interpretation of Bruni and Bracciolini, stressing the figure of the just lawgiver. Brown also notes that it was Machiavelli's portrait — and not those found in the *Collectiones Cosimanae* — which influenced subsequent historical evaluations of the man.

27. "Fu Cosimo, il piú reputato e nomato cittadino, di uomo disarmato, che avesse mai non solamente Firenze ma alcuna altra città di che si abbia memoria: perché non solamente superò ogni altro de' tempi suoi di autorità e di ricchezze ma ancora di liberalità e di prudenza; perché intra tutte le altre qualità che lo feciono principe nella sua patria fu lo essere sopra tutti gli altri uomini liberale e magnifico" (*IF*, p. 458).

28. "E benché queste abitazioni e tutte le altre opere e azioni sue fussero regie e che solo, in Firenze, fusse principe, nondimeno tanto fu temperato dalla prudenza sua che mai la civile modestia non trapassò: perché nelle conversazioni, ne' servidori, nel cavalcare, in tutto il modo del vivere, e ne' parentadi, fu sempre simile a' qualunque modesto cittadino; perché sapeva come le cose estraordinarie che a ogni ora si veggono e appariscono, recono molto piú invidia agli uomini che quelle che sono in fatto e con onestà si ricuoprono" (*IF*, p. 459).

29. "Fu di communale grandezza, di colore ulivigno e di presenza venerabile. Fu sanza dottrina, ma eloquentissimo e ripieno d'una naturale prudenza, e perciò era officioso negli amici, misericordioso ne' poveri, nelle conversazioni utile, ne' consigli cauto, nelle esecuzioni presto, e ne' suoi detti e risposte era arguto e grave" (*IF*, p. 461).

30. "Era meglio città guasta che perduta; e come due canne di panno rosato facevono uno uomo da bene; e che gli stati non si tenevono co' paternostri in mano" (*IF*, pp. 461–62).

31. "Se io, scrivendo le cose fatte da Cosimo, ho imitato quelli che scrivono le vite dei principi, non quelli che scrivono le universali istorie, non ne prenda alcuno ammirazione, perché essendo stato uomo raro nella nostra città, io sono stato necessitato con modo estraordinario lodarlo" (*IF*, p. 463).

32. "Della qual cosa Giuliano de' Medici molte volte con Lorenzo suo fratello si dolfe, dicendo come e' dubitava che, per volere delle cose troppo, che le non si perdessero tutte" (*IF*, p. 511).

33. "Nondimeno Lorenzo, caldo di gioventú e di potenza voleva ad ogni cosa pensare e che ciascuno da lui ogni cosa ricognoscesse. Non potendo adunque i Pazzi con tanta nobiltà e tanta ricchezze sopportare tante ingiurie, cominciorono a pensare come se ne avessero a vendicare" (*IF*, pp. 511–12).

34. "Si vedeva in lui essere due persone diverse, quasi con impossibile congiunzione congiunte" (*IF*, p. 576).

35. This famous letter (*L*, p. 205) will be discussed in another chapter. I have omitted a discussion of Machiavelli's description of Girolamo Savonarola in a letter of 9 March 1498 (*L*, pp. 29–33) which might have been treated in connection with Machiavelli's other portraits of famous Florentines. For detailed discussions of this frequently quoted letter, see Fausto Montanari, *La poesia del Machiavelli* (Rome: Studium, 1953), pp. 64–68, or Allan H. Gilbert, ed. and trans., *The Letters of Machiavelli: A Selection of His Letters* (New York: Capricorn, 1961), pp. 57–61.

36. "Furono nondimeno i portamenti suoi modesti, e in modo contrari alla natura sua, che ciascuno lo amava" (*IF*, p. 182).

37. "Il quale, come vollono i cieli che al male futuro le cose preparavano, arrivò in Firenze in quel tempo appunto che la impresa di Lucca era al tutto perduta" (*IF*, p. 189).

38. "Queste persuasioni accesono lo ambizioso animo del duca di maggiore desiderio del dominare" (*IF*, p. 190).

39. "Per darsi riputazione di severo e di giusto e per questa via accrescersi grazia nella plebe, quegli che avevono amministrata la guerra di Lucca perseguitava; e a messer Giovanni de' Medici, Naddo Rucellai e Guglielmo Altoviti tolse la vita, e molti in esilio e molti in denari ne condennò" (*IF*, p. 190).

40. "Aveva il duca, per dare di sé maggior segno di religione e di umanità, eletto per sua abitazione il convento de' Fra' Minori di Santa Croce" (*IF*, p. 191).

41. "A che noi vi confortiamo ricordandovi che quello domino è solo durabile che è voluntario; né voliate, accecato da un poco di ambizione, condurvi in luogo dove non potendo stare né piú alto salire, siate con massimo danno vostro e nostro di cadere necessitato" (*IF*, p. 194).

42. "Non mossono in alcuna parte queste parole lo indurato animo del duca" (*IF*, p. 194).

43. "Fu questo duca, come i governi suoi dimostrorono, avaro e crudele; nelle udienze difficile, nel rispondere superbo; voleva la servitú, non la benivolenza degli uomini; e per questo piú di essere temuto che amato desiderava" (*IF*, pp. 203–204).

44. "Non era da essere meno odiosa la sua presenza che si fussero i costumi, perché era piccolo, nero, aveva la barba lunga e rada: tanto che da ogni parte di essere odiato meritava, onde che in termine di dieci mesi i

suoi cattivi costumi gli tolsono quella signoria che i cattivi consigli d'altri gli avevono data" (*IF*, p. 204).

Chapter 7

1. Machiavelli originally called the novella simply *Favola*, but it has been traditionally known as *Belfagor archidiavolo o il demonio che prese moglie*, *Belfagor archidiavolo*, or *Belfagor*.

2. "Io ho letto a questi dí *Orlando Furioso* dello Ariosto, et vera-mente il poema è bello tutto, et in di molti luoghi è mirabile. Se si truova costí, raccomandatemi a lui, et ditegli che io mi dolgo solo che, havendo ricordato tanti poeti, che m'habbi lasciato indietro come un cazzo, et ch'egli ha fatto a me quello in sul suo *Orlando*, che io non farò a lui in sul mio *Asino*" (*L*, p. 383).

3. Roberto Ridolfi, *The Life of Niccolò Machiavelli*, trans. Cecil Grayson (Chicago: University of Chicago Press, 1963), p. 175; I use the English translation, which Ridolfi himself (p. ix) prefers to the original edition because of its revisions.

4. J. R. Hale, trans. and ed., *The Literary Works of Machiavelli* (London: Oxford University Press, 1961), p. xv; Hale's enthusiasm for Machiavelli causes him to neglect mention of Petrarch's letters as at least one collection of private correspondence which rivals Machiavelli's letters.

5. Luigi Blasucci, ed., Niccolò Machiavelli, *Opere letterarie* (Milan: Adelphi, 1964), p. xxvi, notes that one of Machiavelli's contemporaries, Matteo Bandello, called him one of the most skillful and prolific storytellers of Tuscany and recounted how Machiavelli once amused a group of dinner guests in 1526 with a humorous tale, one which Bandello himself committed to written form as novella 40 of his *Novelle* on the suggestion of Giovanni de' Medici.

6. Hale, *Literary Works*, p. xi.

7. "Machiavelli in *Belfagor*," *KRQ* 8 (1961): 120–28.

8. *Machiavelli*, p. 158.

9. "L'aspirazione al tragico nelle *Lettere* e nella *Favola*," in *La forma tragica del Principe*, pp. 1–41. Bàrberi Squarotti underlines in *Belfagor* what he calls the problematic relationship of the novella's hero with reality, the "tragic" encounter he has with the diversity and the instability of earthly reality (p. 38).

10. Russo, pp. 160–61, calls Pluto a liberal prince, a perfect republican who could be admitted into the Orti Oricellari circle; Blasucci, p. xxvii, says the speech suggests the portrait of an enlightened despot who deigns to consult his underlings and to submit himself to the law. The *topos* of the infernal council is treated from its classical and Christian origins through the baroque period by O. H. Moore, "The Infernal Council," *MP* 16 (1918–1919): 169–93, and 19 (1921–1922): 47–64. Moore does not mention Machiavelli's use of this literary theme in *Belfagor* and is apparently unaware of its location in the novella.

11. "Ancora che io, dilettissimi miei, per celeste disposizione e

fatale sorte al tutto inrevocabile possegga questo regno, e che per questo io non possa essere obligato ad alcuno iudicio o celeste o mondano, nondimeno, perché gli è maggiore prudenza di quelli che possono piú sottomettersi piú alle leggi e piú stimare l'altrui iudizio: ho deliberato esser consigliato da voi come, in uno caso il quale potrebbe seguire con qualche infamia del nostro imperio, io mi debba governare. Perché dicendo tutte l'anime degli uomini che vengono nel nostro regno esserne stato cagione la moglie, e parendoci questo impossibile, dubitiamo che dando iudizio sopra questa relazione ne possiamo essere calunniati come troppo creduli, e non ne dando come manco severi e poco amatori della iustizia. E perché l'uno peccato è da uomini leggieri e l'altro da ingiusti, e volendo fuggire quegli carichi che da l'uno e l'altro potrebbono dependere, e non trovandone il modo, vi abbiamo chiamati acciò che consigliandone ci aiutiate e siate cagione che questo regno, come per lo passato è vivuto sanza infamia, cosí per lo advenire viva" (*TSL*, pp. 169–70).

12. For a discussion of *ostraneniye* ("making strange"), a central concept of the Russian Formalist critics, see Victor Shklovsky, "Art as Technique" in *Russian Formalist Criticism: Four Essays*, trans. Lee T. Lemon and Marion J. Reis (Lincoln: University of Nebraska Press, 1965), pp. 3–57.

13. "Aveva monna Onesta portato in casa di Roderigo insieme con la nobilità e con la belleza tanta superbia che non ne ebbe mai tanta Lucifero: e Roderigo che aveva provata l'una e l'altra giudicava quella della moglie superiore" (*TSL*, p. 172).

14. "Quegli diavoli, i quali in persona di famigli aveva condotti seco, piú tosto elessono di tornarsene in inferno a stare nel fuoco che vivere nel mondo sotto lo imperio di quella" (*TSL*, p. 173).

15. " 'Oimè, Roderigo mio! Quella è mogliata che ti viene a ritrovare.' Fu cosa maravigliosa a pensare quanta alterazione di mente recassi a Roderigo sentire ricordato il nome della moglie. La quale fu tanta che non pensando s'egli era possibile o ragionevole se la fussi dessa, sanza replicare altro, tutto spaventato se ne fuggí lasciando la fanciulla libera, e volse piú tosto tornarsene in inferno a rendere cagione della sua azioni che di nuovo con tanti fastidii, dispetti e periculi sottoporsi al giogo matrimoniale. E cosí Belfagor tornato in inferno fece fede de' mali che conduceva in una casa la moglie. E Gianmatteo, che ne seppe piú che il diavolo, se ne ritornò tutto lieto a casa" (*TSL*, p. 179).

16. Roberto Ridolfi has recently discovered a manuscript copy of the *Mandragola* in the Laurentian Library's Rediano Codex 129 which dates from 1519 and which mentions the author's name, not found on the first Florentine edition, upon which most editors have based their editions. Ridolfi's subsequent new text, *La Mandragola per la prima volta restituita alla sua integrità* (Florence: Leo S. Olschki, 1965) is, however, not based totally upon this new codex; he simply uses this discovery to correct the printed Florentine edition. Roberto Tissoni, "Per una nuova edizione della *Mandragola* del Machiavelli," *GSLI* 143 (1966): 241–58, rejects Ridolfi's decision not to make a completely new edition. Ridolfi replies in "Ritorno al testo della

Mandragola," in *Studi sulle commedie del Machiavelli* (Pisa: Nistri-Lischi, 1968), pp. 103–34, justifying his choice on the basis that Machiavelli had corrected and revised the edition that was first published and not the manuscript Ridolfi discovered. I have decided to use Gaeta's standard edition rather than Ridolfi's new one in light of this controversy. Other considerations of the problem are to be found in two articles by Fredi Chiappelli, "Sulla composizione della *Mandragola,"* *Approdo* 11 (1965): 79–84, and "Considerazioni di linguaggio e di stile sul testo della *Mandragola,"* *GSLI* 146 (1969): 252–59; and in Anna Stäuble, "Una nuova edizione della *Mandragola* e alcune interpretazioni recenti," *BHR* 27 (1966): 741–43.

17. This argument is found in Theodore A. Sumberg, *"La Mandragola:* An Interpretation," *Journal of Politics* 23 (1961): 320–49, and in Alessandro Parronchi, "La prima rappresentazione della *Mandragola:* il modello per l'apparato — l'allegoria," *Bibliofilia* 64 (1962): 37–86.

18. Franco Fido, "Machiavelli 1469–1969: politica e teatro nel badalucco di Messer Nicia," *Italica* 69 (1969): 359. Fido's article is an excellent summary of the different critical approaches that have been taken to this work.

19. Russo, p. 86.

20. Douglas Radcliff-Umstead, *The Birth of Modern Comedy in Renaissance Italy* (Chicago: University of Chicago Press, 1969), p. 121, notes this aspect of Machiavelli's figures.

21. I agree with Bàrberi Squarotti, *La forma tragica del Principe,* p. 67, who notes that there are no sudden surprises in the play, since human nature is initially defined as evil and undergoes no changes.

22. Radcliff-Umstead, p. 125, notes in passing that Lucrezia says very little and that "knowledge about her is generally gained from other characters." He fails, however, to elaborate on this important observation and does not consider the importance of Ligurio's remark (1.3).

23. Early critics felt that Machiavelli's choice of the name Lucrezia was extremely important and saw her as the Roman matron Lucretia and Nicia as a transfigured Collatinus. Many recent studies now reject this interpretation. Radcliff-Umstead, p. 125, says it is "ironic" but that "Machiavelli does not emphasize the comparison since Nicia is not described as the comic Renaissance equivalent of Collatinus"; Russo, p. 109, also calls it ironic but unimportant. Renzo Sereno, "A Note on the Names of the Personages of Machiavelli's *Mandragola,"* *Italica* 26 (1949): 56, notes the irony but gives far more importance to the etymological meanings of the other characters' names. Livy's account of Lucretia, the symbol of republican virtue and chastity (analogous to Virginia in the story of Appius and Virginus already discussed in reference to the *Discourses*) is found in *Ab urbe condita* (1. 52–59).

24. "E nominò madonna Lucrezia, moglie di messer Nicia Calfucci, alla quale dette tante laude e di bellezze e di costumi che fece restare stupidi qualunche di noi, e in me destò tanto desiderio di vederla che io, lasciato ogni altra deliberazione né pensando piú alle guerre o alla pace di Italia, mi messi

a venire qui: dove arrivato ho trovato la fama di madonna Lucrezia essere minore assai che la verità, il che occorre rarissime volte, e sommi acceso in tanto desiderio d'essere seco che io non truovo loco" (*TSL*, pp. 61–62).

25. "In prima mi fa la guerra la natura di lei che è onestissima e al tutto aliena dalle cose d'amore: . . . in modo che non ci è luogo d'alcuna corruzione" (*TSL*, p. 62).

26. "Bella donna, savia, costumata e atta a governare un regno" (*TSL*, p. 66).

27. "Doppo qualche sospiro disse: 'Poi che l'astuzia tua, la sciocchezza del mio marito, a semplicità di mia madre e la tristizia del mio confessoro mi hanno condotta a fare quello che mai per medesima arei fatto, io voglio iudicare che e' venga da una celeste disposizione che abbi voluto così, e non sono sufficiente a recusare quello che 'l cielo vuole che io accetti. Però io ti prendo per signore, padrone, guida: tu mio padre, tu mio defensore, e tu voglio che sia ogni mio bene; e quello che 'l mio marito ha voluto per una sera, voglio ch'egli abbia sempre" (*TSL*, p. 109).

28. *Machiavelli*, p. 110; Franco Catalano, "Scorci machiavelliani," *NRS*, 49 (1965): 367, agrees, repeating Russo's statement.

29. p. xviii.

30. p. 125.

31. Ibid., p. 137.

32. "Oh Dio, questa vecchiaia ne viene con ogni mal mendo! Ma io non sono ancora sí vecchio che io non rompessi una lancia con Clizia. È egli però possible che io mi sia innamorato a questo modo?" (*TSL*, p. 127).

33. Some critics have noted in passing that scene 4 of Act 2 is a character sketch (Russo, p. 124, and Radcliff-Umstead, p. 139).

34. "Chi conobbe Nicomaco uno anno fa e lo pratica ora, ne debbe restare maravigliato considerando la gran mutazione ch'egli ha fatto. Perché soleva essere uno uomo, grave, resoluto, respettivo. Dispensava el tempo suo onorevolmente. E' si levava la mattina di buon'ora, udiva la sua messa, provedeva al vitto del giorno: dipoi s'egli aveva faccenda in piazza, in mercato, a' magistrati, e' la faceva, quando che no, o e' si riduceva con qualche cittadino tra ragionamenti onorevoli o e' si ritirava in casa nello scrittoio, dove ragguagliava sue scritture, riordinava suoi conti: dipoi piacevolmente con la sua brigata desinava, e desinato ragionava con el figliuolo, ammunivalo, davagli a conoscere gli uomini, e con qualche esempio antico e moderno gl'insegnava vivere: andava dipoi furora, consumava tutto il giorno o in faccende o in diporti gravi e onesti: venuto la sera, sempre l'Avemaria lo trovava in casa: stavasi un poco con esso noi al fuoco s'egli era di verno, dipoi se n'entrava nello scrittoio a rivedere le faccende sue: alle tre ore si cenava allegramente. Questo ordine della sua vita era un esempio a tutti gli altri di casa, e ciascuno si vergognava non lo imitare, e così andavano le cose ordinate e liete" (*TSL*, pp. 132–33).

35. "Ma dapoi che gli entrò questa fantasia di costei, le faccende sue si stracurano, e poderi si guastono, e traffichi rovinano: grida sempre, e non sa di che, entra ed esce di casa ogni dí mille volte senza sapere quello si

vada facendo, non torna mai a ora che si possa cenare o desinare a tempo, se tu gli parli e' non ti risponde o e' ti risponde non a proposito. E servi vedendo questo si fanno beffe di lui, e 'l figliuolo ha posto giú la reverenzia; ognuna fa a suo modo, e infine niuno dubita di fare quello che vede fare a lui. In modo che io dubito, se Iddio non ci rimedia, che questa povera casa non rovini" (*TSL*, p. 133).

36. "Fratel mio, io non so dove io mi fugga, dove io mi nasconda o dove io occulti la gran vergogna della quale io sono incorso. Io sono vituperato in etterno, non ho piú rimedio né potrò mai piú inanzi a mogliama, a' figli, a' parenti, a' servi, capitare. Io ho cerco el vituperio mio, e la mia donna me lo ha aiutato trovare, tanto che io sono spacciato" (*TSL*, p. 159).

37 "Se tu vorrai ritornare al segno, ed essere quel Nicomaco che tu eri da uno anno indrieto, tutti noi vi torneremo e la cosa non si risaprà; e quando ella si risapessi, egli è usanza errare ed amendarsi" (*TSL*, p. 162).

38. "Il modo del rinnovargli è, come è detto, ridurgli verso e' principii suoi. . . . E perché nel processo del tempo quella bontà si corrompe, se non interviene cosa che la riduca al segno, ammazza di necessità quel corpo" (*PD*, p. 379).

39. Russo, p. 115, notes that the soliloquy is Friar Timoteo's typical literary genre; Radcliff-Umstead, p. 129, believes that the friar reveals himself "only in his soliloquies."

40. "Io non so s'abbi giuntato l'un l'altro. Questo tristo di Ligurio ne venne a me con quella prima novella per tentarmi, acciò se io non gliene consentivo non mi arebbe detta questa, per non palesare e disegni loro sanza utile, e di quella che era falsa non si curavono. Egli è vero che io ci sono stato giuntato; nondimeno questo giunto è con mio utile. Messer Nicia e Callimaco son ricchi, e da ciascuno per diversi rispetti sono per trarre assai; la cosa conviene che stia secreta, perché l'importa cosí a loro a dirla come a me. Sia come si voglia, io non me ne pento" (*TSL*, p. 87).

41. Radcliff-Umstead, p. 129.

42. "Voi avete, quanto alla conscienza, a pigliare questa generalità, che dove è un bene certo e un male incerto non si debbe mai lasciare quel bene per paura di quel male. Qui è un bene certo, che voi ingraviderete, acquisterete una anima a messer Domenedio: el male incerto è che colui che iacerà doppo la pozione con voi, si muoia: ma e' si truova anche di quelli che non muoiono. Ma perché la cosa è dubia, però è bene che messer Nicia non corra quel periculo. Quanto all'atto, che sia peccato, questo è una favola, perché la volontà è quella che pecca, non el corpo; e la cagione del peccato è dispiacere al marito, e voi li compiacete; pigliarne piacere, e voi ne avete dispiacere. Oltra di questo, el fine si ha a riguardare in tutte le cose: el fine vostro si è riempiere una sedia in paradiso, contentare il marito vostro. Dice la Bibbia che le figliuole di Lotto, credendosi essere rimase sole nel mondo, usorno con el padre; e, perché la loro intenzione fu buona, non peccorno" (*TSL*, p. 89).

43. "E' dicono el vero quelli che dicono che le cattive compagnie conducono gli uomini alle forche, e molte volte uno càpita male, cosí per

essere troppo facile e troppo buono, come per essere troppo tristo. Dio sa che io non pensavo ad iniurare persona, stavomi nella mia cella, dicevo el mio ufizio, intrattenevo e mia divoti; capitommi inanzi questo diavolo di Ligurio, che mi fece intignere el dito in uno errore, donde io vi ho messo el braccio e tutto la persona, e non so ancora dove io m'abbia a capitare. Pure mi conforto che quando una cosa importa a molti, molti ne hanno a avere cura" (*TSL*, p. 99).

44. "Io non ho potuto questa notte chiudere occhio, tanto è il desiderio che io ho d'intendere come Callimaco e gli altri l'abbino fatto. Ed ho atteso a consumare el tempo in varie cose: io dissi matutino, lessi una vita de' Santi Padri, andai in chiesa ed accesi una lampana che era spenta, mutai uno velo ad una Madonna che fa miracoli. Quante volte ho io detto a questi frati che la tenghino pulita! E si maravigliano poi se la divozione manca. Io mi ricordo esservi cinquecento imagine, e non ve ne sono oggi venti; questo nasce da noi, che non le abbiano saputa mantenere la reputazione. . . . Ora non si fa nulla di queste cose, e po' ci maravigliamo se le cose vanno fredde! Oh, quanto poco cervello è in questi mia frati!" (*TSL*, p. 105).

45. "Io ho udito questo ragionamento e m'è piaciuto, considerando quanto sciocchezza sia in questo dottore; ma la conclusione ultima mi ha sopra modo dilettato. E poiché debbono venire a trovarmi a casa, io non voglio star più qui ma aspettargli alla chiesa, dove la mercanzia varrà più" (*TSL*, pp. 108–109).

46. Martin Fleisher, "Trust and Deceit in Machiavelli's Comedies," *JHI* 26 (1966): 380.

47. *L*, pp. 372–76 (number 163, dated 31 January 1515 and addressed to Francesco Vettori); Giuseppe Velli, "Machiavelli's Letters," *IQ* 6 (1962): 108, feels that "this letter is perhaps superior, for genuine artistic results, to Belfagor's tale."

48. Bruno Basile, "Grotteschi machiavelliani," *Convivium* 34 (1966): 577.

49. "Trovai una vechia che m'imbucatava le camicie, che sta in una casa che è più di meza sottera, né vi si vede lume se non per l'uscio. Et passando io un dí di quivi, la mi riconobbe et, factomi una gran festa, mi disse che io fussi contento andar un poco in casa, che mi voleva mostrare certe camicie belle se io le volevo comperare. Onde io, nuovo cazzo, me lo credetti, et, giunto là, vidi al barlume una donna con uno sciugatoio tra in sul capo et in sul viso che faceva el vergognoso, et stava rimessa in uno canto. Questa vechia ribalda mi prese per mano et menatomi ad colei dixe: 'Questa è la camicia che io vi voglio vendere, ma voglio la proviate prima et poi la pagherete'" (*L*, pp. 204–205). Shklovsky, p. 21, notes that defamiliarization (the basis of *Belfagor*'s structure) is at the center of erotic or sexual euphemisms; in the letters describing Brancacci's adventures or the grotesque prostitute, this technique is frequently used by Machiavelli.

50. "Omè! fu' per cadere in terra morto, tanta era bructa quella femina. E' se le vedeva prima un ciuffo di capelli fra bianchi e neri, cioè canuticci, e benché l'avessi el cocuzolo del capo calvo, per la cui calvitie ad lo scoperto si vedeva passeggiare qualche pidochio, nondimeno e' pochi capelli

e rari le aggiugnevono con le barbe loro fino in su le ciglia; e nel mezzo della testa piccola e grinzosa haveva una margine di fuoco, che la pareva bollata ad la colonna di Mercato; in ogni puncta delle ciglia di verso li occhi haveva un mazetto di peli pieni di lendini; li ochi haveva uno basso et uno alto, et uno era maggiore che l'altro, piene le lagrimatoie di cispa et e' nipitelli dipillicciati; il naso li era conficto sotto la testa aricciato in su, e l'una delle nari tagliata, piene di mocci; la bocca somigliava quella di Lorenzo de' Medici, ma era torta da uno lato e da quello n'usciva un poco di bava, ché per non havere denti non poteva ritenere la scilva; nel labbro di sopra haveva la barba lunghetta, ma rara; el mento haveva lungo aguzato, torto un poco in su, dal quale pendeva un poco di pelle che le adgiugneva infino ad la facella della gola. Stando adtonito ad mirare questo mostro, tucto smarrito, di che lei accortasi volle dire: 'Che havete voi messere?'; ma non lo dixe perché era scilinguata; . . . m'andò tale sdegno ad lo stomaco per non poter sopportare tale offesa, tucto si commosse et commosso operò sí, che io le rece' addosso" (*L*, pp. 205–206).

    51. Amazingly enough, Bàrberi Squarotti applies his search for "tragic" form and language in Machiavelli not only to the letter describing Brancacci's homosexual adventures but also to this grotesque masterpiece in *La forma tragica del Principe*, pp. 13–24, or in "Il Machiavelli fra il 'sublime' della contemplazione intellettuale e il 'comico' della prassi," *LI* 21 (1969): 129–54.

Chapter 8

    1. "E, se vostra Magnificenzia dallo apice della altezza qualche volta volgerà li occhi in questi luoghi bassi, conoscerà quanto io indegnamente sopporti una grande e continua malignità di fortuna" (*PD*, p. 14).

    2. "E se questa materia non è degna / per esser pur leggieri, / d'un uom che voglia parer saggio e grave, / scusatelo con questo, che s'ingegna / con questi van pensieri / fare el suo tristo tempo piú suave, / perch'altrove non have / dove voltare el viso: / ché gli è stato interciso / monstrar con altre imprese altra virtue, / non sendo premio alle fatiche sue" (*TSL*, pp. 57–58).

    3. "Il Machiavelli fra il 'sublime' della contemplazione intellettuale e il 'comico' della prassi," pp. 153–54.

    4. Ibid., p. 130.

    5. "Pure, se io vi potesse parlare, non potre' fare che io non vi empiessi il capo di castellucci, perché la fortuna ha fatto che, non sapendo ragionare né dell'arte della seta, né dell'arte della lana, né de' guadagni né delle perdite, e' mi conviene ragionare dello stato, et mi bisogna o botarmi di stare cheto, a ragionare di questo" (*L*. pp. 239–40).

    6. "Venuta la sera, mi ritorno in casa, et entro nel mio scrittolo; et in su l'uscio mi spoglio quella veste cotidiana, piena di fango et di loto, et mi metto panni reali et curiali; et rivestito condecentemente entro nelle antique corti degli antiqui huomini, dove, da loro ricevuto amorevolmente, mi pasco di quel cibo, che *solum* è mio, e che io nacque per lui; dove io

non mi vergogno parlare con loro, et domandarli della ragione delle loro actioni; et quelli per loro humanità mi rispondono; . . . io ho notato quello di che per la loro conversatione ho fatto capitale, et composto uno opuscolo *De principatibus*" (L, pp. 303–304).

7. "Il Machiavelli fra il 'sublime' della contemplazione intellettuale e il 'comico' della prassi," p. 132.

8. "Humanist Learning in the Renaissance," in *Renaissance Thought 2: Papers on Humanism and the Arts* (New York: Harper, 1965), p. 8.

9. "Chi vedesse le nostre lettere, honorando compare, et vedesse la diversità di quelle, si maraviglierebbe assai, perché gli parrebbe hora che noi fussimo huomini gravi, tutti volti a cose grandi, et che ne' petti nostri non potesse cascare alcuno pensiere che non havesse in sé honestà et grandezza. Però dipoi, voltando carta, gli parrebbe quelli noi medesimi essere leggieri, incostanti, lascivi, volti a cose vane. Questo modo di procedere, se a qualcuno pare sia vituperoso, a me pare laudabile, perché noi imitiamo la natura, che è varia; et chi imita quella non può essere ripreso. Et benché questa varietà noi la solessimo fare in piú lettere, io la voglio fare questa volta in una, come vedrete, se leggerete l'altra faccia. Spurgatevi" (L, p. 374).

10. Francesco Vettori, Florentine ambassador to Rome from 1514 to 1515 and a companion of Machiavelli on his mission to Germany in 1507, was one of Machiavelli's favorite correspondents. Rosemary Devonshire Jones treats their relationships in "Francesco Vettori and Niccolò Machiavelli," *IS* 23 (1968): 93–113.

11. "Né so chosa che dilecti piú a pensarvi e a farlo, che il fottere. E filosofi ogni huomo quanto e' vuole, che questa è la pura verità, la quale molti intendono choxí ma pochi la dichano" (L, p. 372).

12. "Ho lasciato dunque i pensieri delle cose grandi et gravi; non mi diletta piú leggere le cose antiche, né ragionare delle moderne; tutti si sono converse in ragionamenti dolci, di che ringrazio Venere et tutta Cipri" (L, p. 347).

13. *Mimesis: The Representation of Reality in Western Literature*, trans. Willard Trask (Garden City: Doubleday, 1957), pp. 160–61.

14. Ridolfi, *Life of Niccolò Machiavelli*, p. 222, notes that Machiavelli often mystified Guicciardini (who was unfamiliar with poetry) with literary allusions and quotations from memory. In a letter dated 19 December 1525, Machiavelli quoted Dante's *Paradiso* (6. 133–35), and Guicciardini's response of 26 December 1525, is revealing: "You made me look all over Romagna for a copy of Dante . . . and finally I found the text but there was no gloss. I think it must be one of those tricks you always have up your sleeves" (L, p. 448). The contrast is striking. Machiavelli knew Dante well enough to quote even obscure passages from memory; Guicciardini did not even possess a copy of the work and, without a commentary, he was lost.

15. The phrases mean, respectively, "to stoke a fire with stones" and "as the toad said to the harrow."

16. "Quanto alla botta e allo erpice, questo ho invero bisogno di maggior consideratione. Et veramente io ho scartabellato, come fra Timoteo,

di molti libri per ritrovare il fondamento di questo erpice et in fine ho trovarto nel Burchiello un testo che fa molto per me" (*L*, p. 439).

17. "Questo è quanto io ho trovato di buono, et se V. S. ne avesse dubitatione veruna, avvisi" (*L*, p. 440).

18. Ridolfi, *Life of Niccolò Machiavelli*, pp. 174, 304–305, n. 31, points out that some critics have denied that Machiavelli wrote this treatise; see also Hans Baron, "Machiavelli on the Eve of the *Discourses*: The Date and Place of his *Dialogo intorno alla nostra lingua*," *BHR* 23 (1961): 449–76.

19. "Non c'è lingua che si possa chiamare o comune d'Italia o curiale, perché tutte quelle che si potessino chiamare cosí, hanno il fondamento loro dagli scrittori fiorentini e dalla lingua fiorentina" (*TSL*, p. 198). For an examination of Machiavelli's place in the history of the *questione della lingua*, see Cecil Grayson, "Lorenzo, Machiavelli and the Italian Language," in *Italian Renaissance Studies: A Tribute to the Late Cecilia M. Ady*, ed. E. F. Jacobs (London: Faber & Faber, 1960), pp. 410–32. Grayson shows that Machiavelli's argument was aimed not only at Dante but also at Trissino's *Il Castellano della lingua toscana*. Machiavelli knew Trissino's argument — that Dante, Petrarch, and Boccaccio wrote not Florentine but "una lingua eletta, illustre e cortegiana" (Grayson, p. 423) — from Trissino's lectures delivered in Florence in 1513, even though the book was not published until 1529, some fifteen years after Machiavelli's treatise was written. Grayson later altered his opinion on the authorship of the *Dialogo* and now doubts that Machiavelli is the author. For the particulars of his argument, one which uncovers no new evidence and is, to me, unconvincing, see "Machiavelli and Dante," in *Renaissance Studies in Honor of Hans Baron*, ed. Anthony Molho and John A. Tedeschi (DeKalb: Northern Illinois University Press, 1971), pp. 361–84.

20. "Quando questo che io dico sia vero (che è verissimo), io vorrei chiamar Dante chi mi mostrasse il suo poema: . . . Ma perché io voglio parlare un poco con Dante, per fuggire *egli disse* ed *io risposi*, noterò gl'interlocutari davanti" (*TSL*, p. 189).

21. "Dante mio, io voglio che tu t'emendi e che tu consideri meglio il parlar fiorentino e la tua opera" (*TSL*, p. 193).

22. *Life of Niccolò Machiavelli*, p. 175.

23. "Udito che Dante ebbe queste cose le confessò vere e si partí; e io mi restai tutto contento, parendomi d'averlo sgannato" (*TSL*, p. 198).

24. "Io ho, Giuliano, in gamba un paio di geti / con sei tratti di fune in su le spalle: / l'altre miserie mei non vo' contalle, / poiché cosí si trattano e poeti! / Menon pidocchi queste parieti / bolsi spaccati che paion farfalle, / né fu mai tanto puzzo in Roncisvalle / o in Sardigna fra quegli alboreti / quanto nel mio sí delicato ostello" (*TSL*, p. 362, lines 1–9).

25. "Io vi mando, Giuliano, alquanti tordi, / non perché questo don sia buono o bello, / ma perché un po' del pover Machiavello / Vostra Magnificenzia si ricordi" (*TSL*, p. 364, lines 1–4).

26. "Io vi risponderei a tai sermoni, / ch'io son maghero anch'io, come lor sanno, / e spiccon pur di me di buon bocconi" (*TSL*, p. 364, lines 12–14).

Notes

27. Ridolfi, *Life of Niccolò Machiavelli*, pp. 14, 260–61, discusses how artists and sculptors have treated Machiavelli and notes that the di Tito portrait may be a posthumous work made from a death mask.

28. "Poche anime furono come la sua disposte all'apprensione dei contrasti, a ricevere piú profondamente l'impressione delle incongruenze della vita." Cited from Luigi Pirandello, *Saggi, Poesie, Scritti vari*, ed. Manlio lo Vecchio-Musti (Milan: Mondadori, 1960), p. 109.

29. "Io ero in sul cesso quando arrivò il vostro messo, et appunto pensavo alle stravaganze di questo mondo, et tutto ero volto a figurarmi un predicatore a mio modo per a Firenze, et fosse tale quale piacesse a me, perché in questo voglio essere caparbio come nelle altre oppinioni mie. . . . Vero è che io so che io sono contrario, come in molte altre cose, all'oppinione di quelli cittadini: eglino vorrieno un predicatore che insegnasse loro la via del Paradiso, et io vorrei trovarne uno che insegnassi loro la via di andare a casa il diavolo; vorrebbono appresso che fosse huomo prudente, intero reale, et io ne vorrei uno piú pazzo che il Ponzo, piú versuto che fra Girolamo, piú ippocrito che frate Alberto, perché mi parrebbe una bella cosa, et degna della bontà di questi tempi, che tutto quello che noi habbiamo sperimentato in molti frati, si esperimentasse in uno; perché io credo che questo sarebbe il vero modo ad andare in Paradiso: inparare la via dello Inferno per fuggirla" (*L*, pp. 402–403).

30. This phrase, referring to the clogs or sandals worn by the friars, is found in a letter from Guicciardini dated 18 May 1521 (*L*, p. 407).

31. "Machiavello carissimo. Quando io leggo i vostri titoli di oratori di Repubblica et di frati et considero con quanti Re, Duchi et Principi voi havete altre volte negoziato, mi ricordi di Lysandro, a chi doppo tante victorie et trophei fu dato la cura di distribuire la carne a quelli medesimi soldati a chi sí gloriosamente haveva comandato; et dico: Vedi che, mutati *solum* e' visi delli huomini et i colori extrinseci, le cose medesime tucte ritornano; né vediamo accidente alcuno che a altri tempi non sia stato veduto. Ma el mutare nomi et figura alle cose fa che soli e' prudenti le riconoschono" (*L*, p. 407). Guicciardini's reference to a belief in a constant recurrence of historical events based on the implicit premise that man's nature is constant has a Machiavellian ring and is similar to another statement in Guicciardini's *Ricordi*, number 76 in *Francesco Guicciardini: Opere*, ed. Di Vittorio de Caprariis (Milan: Mondadori, 1953), p. 113: "Everything that has been in the past and is at present will be in the future; but the names and appearances change such that whoever does not have a keen eye does not recognize this, nor does he know how to make of this observation a basis for rules of conduct or judgment." However, Guicciardini elsewhere underlined the importance of the *particolare*, the particular fact rather than the general, abstract rule as in *Ricordi* 6: "It is a great mistake to talk of things indiscriminately and absolutely and, in other words, by rules" (*Opere*, p. 98), or more importantly, in *Ricordi* 110, where he implicitly rejects Machiavelli's exemplary Romans: "How mistaken are those who quote the Romans with every word" (*Opere*, p. 120).

32. *Life of Niccolò Machiavelli*, p. 194.

Chapter 9

1. Scholes and Kellogg, *The Nature of Narrative*, p. 161.

2. Wilcox, *The Development of Florentine Humanist Historiography*, underlines the "complete absence of physical characterization" in Bruni's works (p. 58), but sees that Machiavelli "successfully incorporates sensory elements and provides a more convincing picture of the event" (p. 203).

3. Plutarch's statement — "It must be borne in mind that my design is not to write histories, but lives" — is found in the opening paragraph of his comparison of Alexander and Caesar on p. 801 of the previously cited Dryden translation.

4. See E. I. McQueen, "Quintus Curtius Rufus," in *Latin Biography*, ed. T. A. Dorey (New York: Basic Books, 1967), pp. 17–18, for this distinction between classical history and biography.

5. See Scholes and Kellogg, p. 165; or A. J. Gossage, "Plutarch," in *Latin Biography*, p. 66.

6. I owe this succinct description to Gossage, ibid.

7. For an excellent discussion of characterization in Homeric epic, see Scholes and Kellogg, pp. 161–65.

8. The quotation — "Quanto piace al mondo è breve sogno" — is taken from the first poem in Petrarch's *Canzoniere*, "Voi ch'ascoltate in rime sparse il suono" (line 14).

9. "Io spero e lo sperar cresce 'l tormento, / io piango e il pianger ciba il lasso core, / io rido e el rider mio non passa drento, / io ardo e l'arsion non par di fore, / io temo ciò che io veggo e ciò che io sento, / ogni cosa mi dà nuovo dolore: / così sperando, piango, rido e ardo, / e paura ho di ciò che io odo e guardo" (*TSL*, p. 357).

10. In his *Life and Times of Niccolò Machiavelli*, trans. Linda Villari (New York: Scribner's, 1898), p. 504, Pasquale Villari suggests that this dream could have been manufactured by Pagolo Giovio, whose *Elogia clarorum virorum* (Venice, 1546) sharply criticized Machiavelli's works on moral grounds.

11. See Ridolfi, *Life of Niccolò Machiavelli*, pp. 249–50, for a fuller discussion of this dream and the problem of its authenticity.

12. A reference to this deathbed confession is found in a letter from Piero Machiavelli to Francesco Nelli written on 22 June 1527 (*L*, p. 509). The authenticity of this letter has been questioned by Eugenia Levi, "Nota su di un falso Machiavelliano," *Pensiero politico* 2 (1969): 459–63.

13. "Of so great a name no praise is sufficient." Villari, p. 508, notes that this monument was placed over Machiavelli's tomb in the church of Santa Croce in Florence in the eighteenth century through the efforts of a public subscription sponsored by George Nassau Clavering, third Earl Cowper (an ardent Italophile and an honorary citizen of Florence) and the Grand Duke of Tuscany. Villari's work also contains an excellent photograph of the monument with its inscription.

Index

Peter E. Bondanella is assistant professor of Italian at Indiana University. He received his A.B. degree (1966) in French and political science at Davidson College, his M.A. degree (1967) in political science at Stanford University, and his Ph.D. (1970) in comparative literature from the University of Oregon. He has published numerous articles on Renaissance literature.

The manuscript was edited by Linda Grant. The book was designed by Joanne Kinney. The typeface for the text is Electra designed by W. A. Dwiggins about 1935; and the display face is Garamont designed by Claude Garamond in the 16th century.

The text is printed on Special Book Litho paper; and the book is bound in Columbia Mills Llamique cloth over binders boards. Manufactured in the United States of America.